Refuge

DEVOTIONS FOR FINDING STRENGTH AND COMFORT

RON MOORE

THE
JOURNEY™
with Ron Moore

© 2016 by Ron Moore

Back to the Bible Editor: Michael Ross
Proofreader: Laura Gross

ISBN 978-1-942464-29-7

Refuge

DEVOTIONS FOR
FINDING STRENGTH
AND COMFORT

Contents

GOD WILL FIGHT FOR YOU

Exodus 14:14
"The LORD himself will fight for you. Just stay calm."

The twins of fear and doubt roll in like thirty-foot waves and crash onto the shores of our souls. They produce anxiety that leads to more fear and "what if" questions that lead to doubt.

Fresh from being delivered out of slavery, the Israelites were caught between the powerful Egyptians and the Red Sea. No wonder they were terrified and cried out, "It would have been better for us to serve the Egyptians than to die in the desert!" (NIV). Moses calmed them with these words, "Do not be afraid. Stand firm and you will see the deliverance the LORD will bring you today … The LORD will fight for you; you need only to be still" (NIV). You know the rest of the story.

Here they come rolling in, the waves of fear and doubt, caused by sickness, job loss, a relationship breakup, illness of a loved one, discouragement, death. You can't stand up under the force of the crashing waves. You don't have to. The Lord will absorb the powerful force for you. You need only to be still.

Lord, I want to stand firm, but there are times when fear takes over. I want to live with faith, but there are times when doubt bursts through the door of my heart. O Father, help me to be still and watch you fight the battle for me. In Jesus' name. Amen.

Personal Reflection:

_____

_____

_____

_____

_____

_____

_____

_____

_____

_____

_____

_____

_____

_____

_____

_____

_____

_____

_____

_____

_____

_____

SAFE AND SECURE

Leviticus 26:9-13

"I will look favorably upon you, making you fertile and multiplying your people. And I will fulfill my covenant with you. You will have such a surplus of crops that you will need to clear out the old grain to make room for the new harvest! I will live among you, and I will not despise you. I will walk among you; I will be your God, and you will be my people. I am the LORD your God, who brought you out of the land of Egypt so you would no longer be their slaves. I broke the yoke of slavery from your neck so you can walk with your heads held high."

What makes you feel secure? Where do you go for safety? What makes you smile a smile of confidence? What delivers a settled peace in your soul? Here's what some people cling to.

- **RELATIONSHIPS.** Sooner or later people will let you down.

- **INTIMACY.** A short-term fix that leaves you emptier than before the fling.

- **CAREERS.** Ever heard of "economic downturn" or "downsizing"?

- **401K.** Take a ride on the roller coaster of the stock market and quarterly business reports.

- **SUBSTANCE.** Enjoy the short high. The long low is a bummer.

- **YOURSELF.** "I am the Captain of my soul!" Really? Good luck with that.

I love today's passage because it reminds me of an all-important truth: God is the only source of true security. With our lives committed to Jesus Christ and our faith and trust securely in him, we are forgiven and free. We have been freed from the slavery of sin … and saved from the sting of death. (See 1 Corinthians 15:55-57.) We can walk through this life with our heads held high—joyfully awaiting the promise of eternal life with God!

Father, thank you for breaking the yoke of slavery. Thank you for delivering me from sin. Thank you for giving me eternal life! In the name of my Lord and Savior Jesus Christ. Amen.

Personal Reflection:

A WAY THROUGH FEAR

Numbers 6:24-26
*"May the LORD bless you and protect you. May the LORD
smile on you and be gracious to you. May the LORD
show you his favor and give you his peace."*

Sometimes fear is physical. When the big black dog that lives down
the road comes after me during my morning run, I am physically
affected. Even though his owner has him on a leash, the growling,
barking, lunging, and baring of teeth does something to the beat of
my heart and the speed of my pace.

Many times fear is mental. It swirls in our minds with questions
like "What if the job goes away?" "What if the tests show cancer?"
"What if the surgery isn't successful?" "What if the treatment
doesn't stop the spread?" "What if he leaves?" "What if I am not
reconciled with my child?"

All those "what if" scenarios have a way of trapping us in a prison of
fear. Yet we can escape. In times of trouble, the Lord gives us what
we so desperately need: comfort, protection, peace—a way through
fear. Relief comes when we get our minds off "what if" and focus on
"The One Who Can." While turmoil is inevitable, we have hope in
our Lord Jesus Christ. Can you sense his smile on your life … his
graciousness? Perhaps not in the grip of fear, but hold steady. He
will restore peace.

*Father, it is so easy to keep our sights on the storm. We need your
help to keep our minds steadfast and trusting in you. Keep us
anchored to you — the Rock eternal. In Jesus' name. Amen.*

Personal Reflection:

THE LORD IS WITH US

Numbers 14:8-9
"And if the LORD is pleased with us, he will bring us safely into that land and give it to us. It is a rich land flowing with milk and honey. Do not rebel against the LORD, and don't be afraid of the people of the land. They are only helpless prey to us! They have no protection, but the LORD is with us! Don't be afraid of them!"

The people of Israel were free from the slavery of Egypt, but they were not free from the slavery of fear. After exploring the Promised Land, the majority reported, "We can't attack those people; they are stronger than we are. We seemed like grasshoppers in our own eyes, and we looked the same to them" (NIV). Only two men contradicted the reports.

Joshua and Caleb had a different spirit. They followed the Lord wholeheartedly. They pleaded with the people to obey God and follow him into the land of Canaan. They were certain that God would defeat the enemy no matter how big or how many. They said with confidence, "The LORD is with us! Don't be afraid ..." Unfortunately, the people followed the majority and, as a result, died wandering in the desert. Only Joshua and Caleb entered the Land of Promise.

Living without fear allows you to embrace the promises of God. Instead of paralysis, you can move forward in God's strength and power. Your "enemies" surround you—illness, uncertainty, job loss, grief, relationship struggles. Many challenges in life seem bigger than you are. In fact, they *are* bigger than you are! However, they are not bigger than the God you serve. The Lord is with you! Don't be afraid!

Father, don't let us shrink back in fear and miss your promises. Give us spirits like Joshua and Caleb. Help us follow you wholeheartedly. Help us follow you with confidence. In Jesus' name. Amen.

Personal Reflection:

_____

_____

_____

_____

_____

_____

_____

_____

_____

_____

_____

_____

_____

_____

_____

_____

_____

_____

HE WILL NEVER ABANDON YOU

Deuteronomy 31:6

"So be strong and courageous! Do not be afraid and do not panic before them. For the LORD your God will personally go ahead of you. He will neither fail you nor abandon you."

Fear is real and unrelenting. When you feel like you've conquered "Fear A," the thrill of victory is soon replaced by the agony of defeat from "Fear B." While anxiety visits us all, it is a permanent houseguest for some. The question is not "Will anxiety come?" The question is "What will I do with the fear when it arrives?"

Today's passage answers the question. Moses was now 120 years old and knew the time had come to let Joshua lead. Up to this point, the journey into the Promised Land had been long, slow, painful, and even downright scary at times. Danger surrounded them. Yet Moses knew his successor could handle the assignment … that is, if he heeded some godly wisdom. "Be strong and courageous!" he told Joshua with all of Israel watching. "Do not be afraid or discouraged, for the LORD will personally go ahead of you. He will be with you; he will neither fail you nor abandon you" (Deuteronomy 31:8).

Are you willing to give your fears to God and trust that he will take care of you? The Lord is omniscient, so he knows what to do with the challenges you face. He's omnipotent, so he is able to take care of the situation. Anxiety weighs us down and wears us out. Give it to God. He loves you so much that he doesn't want you to stumble under the weight. He will carry it as he walks by your side. He will even go ahead of you … but will never ever fail nor abandon you. Do you believe this?

Father, thank you for this great invitation. Remind me of your invitation often when anxiety overtakes me. Whisper in my ear, "Give it to me." Give me the strength and wisdom to let you have it all. In Jesus' name. Amen.

Personal Reflection:

_____

_____

_____

_____

_____

_____

_____

_____

_____

_____

_____

_____

_____

_____

_____

_____

_____

_____

THE ROCK

Deuteronomy 32:4
*"He is the Rock; his deeds are perfect. Everything he does is just
and fair. He is a faithful God who does no wrong;
how just and upright he is!"*

God's righteousness means that he always acts in accordance with
what is right and is himself the final standard of what is right. God
is perfect and all his actions are perfect. He is just in all he does.
God can never think, desire, or do evil. He does no wrong.

Years ago I ran across this old song. The text was written by a German
teacher, Samuel Rodigast. He wrote these words to encourage a
very sick friend. Let this be today's prayer.

*Whate'er my God ordains is right, His holy will abideth; I will be
still whate'er He doth, And follow where He guideth. He is my God,
Though dark my road, He holds me that I shall not fall,
Wherefore to Him I leave it all.*

*Whate'er my God ordains is right, He never will deceive me;
He leads me by the proper path, I know He will not leave me,
And take content What He hath sent; His hand can turn
my griefs away, And patiently I wait His day.*

*Whate'er my God ordains is right, Here shall my stand be taken;
Though sorrow, need, or death be mine, Yet am I not forsaken,
My Father's care Is round me there, He holds me that
I shall not fall, And so to Him I leave it all.*

Personal Reflection:

GOD IS WITH YOU

Joshua 1:9
"This is my command—be strong and courageous!
Do not be afraid or discouraged. For the LORD
your God is with you wherever you go."

The weight was heavy! Since his youth, Joshua had followed the great Moses. Scripture says that no one ever demonstrated the "mighty power or performed the awesome deeds" that Moses did (Deuteronomy 34:12 NIV). However, Moses was dead. Now the assignment of leading Israel into the Promised Land was heavy on Joshua's shoulders.

Maybe you are carrying your own burden today. God has given you a difficult assignment. Illness, grief, loss, fear and/or anxiety weigh down your heart. It is a load that never leaves. The mission is yours to carry out and you feel alone, even when surrounded by people.

Read today's passage. Read it again. God's instruction is clear: "Be strong!" "Be courageous!" "Don't be afraid!" "Do not be discouraged!" However, God's instruction is not without a foundation. In fact, he is the foundation! Wherever you go, whatever you're going through, whenever you are afraid, he is right there with you. He will never leave nor forsake you. Strength, courage, and freedom from fear are found in him alone. He will give you everything you need to do what he is calling you to do.

Lord, I can't carry the weight alone. Thank you for the promise of
your presence. Thank you for the power of your presence. Right now
I am giving my burden to you. When I take it back, remind me that
you want to carry it for me. In Jesus' name. Amen.

Personal Reflection:

_____

_____

_____

_____

_____

_____

_____

_____

_____

_____

_____

_____

_____

_____

_____

_____

_____

_____

_____

_____

_____

NOTHING CAN HINDER THE LORD

1 Samuel 14:6

"Let's go across to the outpost of those pagans," Jonathan said to his armor bearer. "Perhaps the LORD will help us, for nothing can hinder the LORD. He can win a battle whether he has many warriors or only a few!"

King Saul was in trouble. He was outnumbered by the Philistine army, who held the high ground, and so he froze. He and his men took their position under a pomegranate tree. There he waited ... and waited ... and waited ... but his son Jonathan couldn't wait any longer.

Without his father's knowledge, Jonathan decided to take matters into his own hands. His confidence in God's deliverance is declared in today's passage—"Nothing can hinder the Lord from saving, whether by many or by few" (NIV). After seeking God's direction, Jonathan climbed up to the Philistines and, with his armor bearer, killed 20 enemy soldiers. Then God rewarded his faith. Panic struck the whole Philistine army. "It was a panic sent by God" (1 Samuel 14:15 NIV).

Living without fear will not allow you to sit frozen under your "pomegranate tree." You will be compelled to move forward in God's will and face your circumstance. When God is on your side, nothing can hinder him from delivering you regardless of the challenge. Now, move out from under the tree and watch God work in your life!

Father, don't let us sit frozen under our "pomegranate tree" of fear. Help us to move forward with the confidence that nothing, absolutely nothing, can hinder you from accomplishing your will in our lives. In Jesus' name. Amen.

Personal Reflection:

_____

_____

_____

_____

_____

_____

_____

_____

_____

_____

_____

_____

_____

_____

_____

_____

_____

_____

_____

_____

_____

THE BATTLE IS THE LORD'S

1 Samuel 17:45,47

David replied to the Philistine, "You come to me with sword, spear, and javelin, but I come to you in the name of the LORD of Heaven's Armies—the God of the armies of Israel, whom you have defiled. … And everyone assembled here will know that the LORD rescues his people, but not with sword and spear. This is the LORD's battle, and he will give you to us!"

King Saul and all his men "were dismayed and terrified" (NIV). A nine-feet-tall giant named Goliath challenged the Israelite army day after day to a one-on-one battle, winner take all. After 40 days, no one had stepped forward. The soldiers were frozen with fear.

On day 41 a young boy named David came to deliver some food to his three brothers who were serving in the army. When he heard Goliath's challenges he was incensed that a "Philistine … is allowed to defy the armies of the living God" (NIV). David stepped forward. He faced Goliath with only a sling and five stones, and planted his first shot right in the middle of the giant's forehead.

Living without fear means that we face our giants, and everyone has a giant or two. Our giants stand before us "with sword, spear, and javelin" (NIV), armed to the hilt; but we can face them in the name of the Lord Almighty. Standing alone, you are no match for your giant, but God is the One who saves. Remember, your battle belongs to the Lord. Read that amazing truth one more time … YOUR BATTLE BELONGS TO THE LORD!

Father, help that truth sink deep into my heart. So often I am frozen with fear as I face my personal giants. Remind me that the battle belongs to you. Help me move forward without fear. In Jesus' name. Amen.

Personal Reflection:

_____

_____

_____

_____

_____

_____

_____

_____

_____

_____

_____

_____

_____

_____

_____

_____

PERFECT

2 Samuel 22:31

"God's way is perfect. All the LORD's promises prove true. He is a shield for all who look to him for protection."

God never makes a mistake. He never needs a mulligan. He never asks for a do-over. His instruction is impeccable. His plans are perfect. His future for you is faultless. Our confidence is in knowing that God shields us as we run to him for refuge in times of trial.

Challenging times are not the only way our faith can be exercised and our confidence increased. George Mueller reminds us that the daily reading of God's flawless Word is essential for learning and experiencing God's character. Mueller writes,

> *There is the reading of the Scriptures, that we may by them acquaint ourselves with God as He has revealed Himself in His Word.*
>
> *Are you able to say, from the acquaintance you have made with God, that He is a lovely Being? If not, let me affectionately entreat you to ask God to bring you to this, that you may admire His gentleness and kindness, that you may be able to say how good He is, and what a delight it is to the heart of God to do good to His children.*

Take the time to read God's Word and learn that he is, indeed, a "lovely Being." Then, when you run to him for refuge, you'll be able to experience what you have learned.

*Father, give us the desire to read your flawless Word and learn
that your way is perfect before we need to experience that truth in
challenging times. In Jesus' name. Amen.*

Personal Reflection:

_____

_____

_____

_____

_____

_____

_____

_____

_____

_____

_____

_____

_____

_____

_____

_____

_____

_____

_____

COURAGE

2 Samuel 22:32
*"For who is God except the LORD? Who but
our God is a solid rock?"*

When we place our trust and confidence in people, sooner or later we will be left alone and disillusioned. When we seek satisfaction in stuff, our hearts will crash like a person coming down from a heroin high. When we worship money, we run after a god who never quite quenches our thirst. False gods always leave us alone and afraid.

As Alexis de Tocqueville recorded his famous observations on America in the 1830s, he wrote of a "strange melancholy that haunts the inhabitants … in the midst of abundance." Americans believed, and still believe, that prosperity brings happiness but, as de Tocqueville noted, "the incomplete joys of this world will never satisfy [the human] heart" (Tim Keller, *Counterfeit Gods*).

David reminds us in today's passage that there is no God besides the LORD! There is no steady and secure refuge except the Rock! He alone is the remedy for the "strange melancholy" that infects our natural hearts. He alone fills our fearful hearts with courage.

Father, show us where our fear is a "reward" for the false gods we chase. Help us turn from the gods that leave us alone and afraid, and run to you — the Rock. In Jesus' name. Amen.

Personal Reflection:

_____

_____

_____

_____

_____

_____

_____

_____

_____

_____

_____

_____

_____

_____

_____

_____

_____

_____

_____

_____

_____

_____

ARMED WITH STRENGTH

2 Samuel 22:33
"God is my strong fortress, and he makes my way perfect."

Perpetua was a 26-year-old mother with a nursing baby when she was imprisoned for refusing to bow before idols. Despite her father appearing with the infant in his arms and pleading for her to sacrifice to idols, she refused. "Are you a Christian?" the judge asked. "I am a Christian," was her answer. Perpetua was ordered to be killed by wild beasts.

As the young woman entered the arena, she sang a hymn of triumph. Several men were torn to pieces by leopards and bears. Perpetua and another young woman were stripped of their clothes and hung up in nets to be gored by a bull. When the bull failed to kill her, gladiators were given the task. "Perpetua was assigned to a trembling young man who stabbed her weakly several times ... When she saw how upset the young man was, Perpetua guided his sword to a vital area and died" (John Foxe, *Christian Martyrs of the World*, pgs. 12-14).

The same God who armed Perpetua with supernatural strength in AD 200 is the same God who arms us with strength today. Our battle may not be in an arena of martyrdom, but we need God to arm us with strength nonetheless. Disease, discouragement, and depression take their stabs at our hearts. Fear will come at us like a hungry leopard and tear at our souls, but God is there to arm us with strength and keep our way safe and protected. With him on your side, you can go through each day singing a hymn of triumph.

Father, on our own we are afraid and weak. Arm us with your strength. Remind us often today that when we are walking with you, our way is always secure. In Jesus' name. Amen.

Personal Reflection:

THE LORD—HE IS GOD

1 Kings 18:37-39

"O LORD, answer me! Answer me so these people will know that you, O LORD, are God and that you have brought them back to yourself." Immediately the fire of the LORD flashed down from heaven and burned up the young bull, the wood, the stones, and the dust. It even licked up all the water in the trench! And when all the people saw it, they fell face down on the ground and cried out, "The LORD—he is God! Yes, the LORD is God!"

When the prophet Elijah learned that the people had abandoned God's instruction and were following other gods, he called a meeting on Mount Carmel. Elijah went before the people and said, "How long will you waver between two opinions? If the Lord is God, follow him; but if Baal is God, follow him" (NIV). Then Elijah challenged the prophets of Baal to a duel.

Two piles of wood were set up and a sacrifice prepared. The god who lit the pile of wood would prove to be the real God. Baal's prophets called on their god from morning till noon. They cut themselves until their blood flowed. They continued their pleas until evening, but there was no response. Then Elijah took his turn. After having the wood soaked with water, he called on the Lord. "Then the fire of the Lord fell!" The people cried, "The Lord—he is God! The Lord—he is God!"(NIV).

Do you have any "gods" in your life? Do you have things that tug at your heart or even turn it in the wrong direction? Living without fear allows us to face those "gods" that stand in the way of following the Lord wholeheartedly. If you are running away from God, it's time to stop and turn your heart back to him again.

Father, we acknowledge you as the only God. Forgive us for chasing after other "gods" that give us a short and shallow satisfaction. Help us turn our hearts back to you. In Jesus' name. Amen.

Personal Reflection:

DO THE WORK

1 Chronicles 28:20
Then David continued, "Be strong and courageous, and do the work. Don't be afraid or discouraged, for the LORD God, my God, is with you. He will not fail you or forsake you. He will see to it that all the work related to the Temple of the LORD is finished correctly."

When we walk with God, failure is not possible. Surely we can fail, but God never fails us. Since he is with us, he will give us his success and turn our missteps into learning experiences.

Solomon had some serious challenges ahead of him, but David's charge to him was "Be strong and courageous, and do the work." Solomon could set aside fear and discouragement because the personal God who never fails nor forsakes was with him. God would ensure that Solomon's work on the temple would not fail, but be finished.

We have the same promise. God is with us! He is our God and he is with us. He will never fail us. He will never forsake us. The good work he started in us will be finished in his timing and according to his will. Be strong and courageous, and press on to do the work that God has for you to do.

Lord Jesus, thank you for always being with us. Thank you that you will never leave us, forsake us, or fail us. Amen.

Personal Reflection:

_____

_____

_____

_____

_____

_____

_____

_____

_____

_____

_____

_____

_____

_____

_____

_____

_____

_____

_____

_____

_____

LIFTED TO SAFETY

Job 5:10-11

"He gives rain for the earth and water for the fields. He gives prosperity to the poor and protects those who suffer."

Maybe you have lost a loved one. Maybe you have lost your health. Maybe you have relocated and left good friends behind. Maybe the love of your life has left you behind. Grief is the response to the different forms of loss. While it feels foreign, it is a normal and expected response. Moving through mourning is a process that can make progress only when our eyes are on the Lord.

Look around you and see the work of God. He provides the needed water for plants and crops and the flowers highlighting the countryside. If he cares that much for the plants, how much more does he care for you!

Grief is natural, but God responds to us in a supernatural way. He never leaves us alone. He never abandons us. He gives us what we need right when we need it. He meets us right where we are but doesn't leave us there. He reaches down to those feeling low and lifts them up. He embraces those who are mourning and brings them to safety. Look up! He is reaching out to you!

Father, someone reading this is very low. Please lift them up. Someone else reading this is in the pit of grief. Please lift them to safety. Please do your supernatural work. In Jesus' name. Amen.

Personal Reflection:

_____

_____

_____

_____

_____

_____

_____

_____

_____

_____

_____

_____

_____

_____

_____

_____

_____

_____

_____

_____

_____

_____

_____

PERFECT KNOWLEDGE

Job 37:16

*"Do you understand how he moves the clouds with
wonderful perfection and skill?"*

God's knowledge is universal. God knows everything there is to
know about everything there is to know. God's knowledge of all
things is complete. He doesn't need to study; there is nothing for
him to learn. He knows what will happen tomorrow and 100 years
from tomorrow.

God's knowledge is personal. God knows everything there is to
know about you. He knows how much you love him and how you
desire to please him. He knows your weaknesses and the sins that
trip you up. He knows the secret sins you thought were hidden
deep in your heart. He knows your worst thought and your greatest
fear, and loves you anyway.

God's knowledge is unconditional. Think of it! He knows everything
about you and loves you anyway. He sent his Son to make you his
child. His knowledge about you doesn't cause him to turn away
from you. He promises that nothing can separate you from his love.
God knows you intimately and loves you deeply. There is no need
to hide what's on your heart.

*Father, it's an amazing truth that you, who know all of our desires,
thoughts, and fears, still love us. Thank you for your amazing love.
In Jesus' name. Amen.*

Personal Reflection:

_____

_____

_____

_____

_____

_____

_____

_____

_____

_____

_____

_____

_____

_____

_____

_____

_____

_____

_____

_____

_____

_____

EYES ON THE LORD

Psalm 16:7-8

I will bless the LORD who guides me; even at night my heart instructs me. I know the LORD is always with me. I will not be shaken, for he is right beside me.

Do you ever have nights when you can't go to sleep? You toss and turn and your mind begins to race. Then fear shows up. For those of you going through times of illness, nights can be the worst. While others sleep, nights are a lonely time that invite your mind to entertain all the "what ifs," and "what ifs" never bring comfort.

In today's passage the writer knows about the fear of night, but he has learned a calming secret. When aloneness came, he was determined to keep his eyes on the Lord. He read and reflected on his Word. He repeated comforting and encouraging passages. He knew that when God was at his right hand, he would not and could not be shaken.

When our eyes are on our challenge, self-counsel takes over. Self-counsel opens the door for fear to walk in unchecked. However, when our focus is on Jesus, the psalmist says that he is the One "who guides me." Even when we are alone, "even at night," the heart focused on Jesus gives us comforting and encouraging instruction.

Father, lonely times are times when our minds can wander. We pray that lonely times will be our reminder to meet with you. With you at our side, we will not be shaken. With you at our side, our hearts will give us good counsel, even at night. Thank you in Jesus' name. Amen.

Personal Reflection:

_____

_____

_____

_____

_____

_____

_____

_____

_____

_____

_____

_____

_____

_____

_____

_____

_____

_____

_____

_____

_____

MY ROCK, MY SAVIOR

Psalm 18:1-2

*I love you, LORD; you are my strength. The LORD is my rock,
my fortress, and my savior; my God is my rock,
in whom I find protection. He is my shield, the power that
saves me, and my place of safety.*

The prophet Samuel had anointed David as the new king of Israel. However, Saul, the reigning king, did not read the email blast. The king God had rejected was obsessed with killing the competition. Saul and his best soldiers were chasing David around the countryside. After a close call, David wrote the words in today's passage thanking God for delivering him.

He declares the Lord as his:

- Strength—David knows the energy to keep going comes from God.

- Rock—God is a great boulder that we can hide behind in life's fierce storms.

- Fortress—Think high, thick, impenetrable walls. Think protection.

- Shield—This defensive armor deflects all the flaming arrows of the devil.

- Power—Only he has the power to defeat death and give us eternal life.

- Savior—Ultimately God liberates us and brings freedom.

Psalm 18 was not the last time that God delivered David from Saul, but David lived one day at a time declaring the great attributes of his great God. So can you.

Father, thank you for today's strength, protection, and deliverance. I'll be back tomorrow in need of the same things. In Jesus' name. Amen.

Personal Reflection:

_____

_____

_____

_____

_____

_____

_____

_____

_____

_____

_____

_____

_____

_____

_____

CLEAN AND CLEAR

Psalm 19:9
*Reverence for the LORD is pure, lasting forever. The laws
of the LORD are true; each one is fair.*

We are most disturbed in disobedience. When our will has its back turned on God, chaos reigns. When we've decided that our way is best, anxiety is amplified. On any road trip away from God, our personal fear rides shotgun.

The fear of the Lord is different. Reread today's passage. The fear of the Lord is clean. Like a mountain spring the fear of the Lord is a flow of fresh honor and respect confirmed by refreshing obedience. The unpolluted life continues as we choose to walk with God.

Let me ask a question. Could it be that you are living in fear because you're not following God? Could it be that peace won't come because practical obedience isn't the pattern of your life? Could it be that disobedience is producing the dread in your heart? Maybe it's time to come home. On the road back, God will drive. You'll ride shotgun, and personal fear will be packed in the trunk.

*Search me, O God, and show me my heart; test me and bring my
anxious thoughts to the surface. Reveal my offensive ways and lead
me in a path of purity that lasts forever. In Jesus' name. Amen.*

Personal Reflection:

_____

_____

_____

_____

_____

_____

_____

_____

_____

_____

_____

_____

_____

_____

_____

_____

_____

_____

_____

_____

_____

_____

TRUST

Psalm 20:7

Some nations boast of their chariots and horses, but we boast in the name of the LORD our God.

Some people like to trust in tangible stuff. Things they can see and touch, such as a strong showing of the Dow, a large and equipped military, a secure retirement, their party running the government. Some trust in fast, fortified chariots pulled by strong, speedy horses

For the believer, tangible things are to be used, not worshiped. God calls us to trust him in all things. Things of this world will rust, rot, and decay. He is the only One who is the same from eternity past to eternity future.

What are you trusting in? What makes confidence well up inside you? What do you look toward and cling to regardless of whether the stocks are up or down? One day he will be the only One there is to trust.

Father, help us trust in you alone regardless of the times, our health, or our job situations. Don't let us allow anything to supplant our trust in you alone. In Jesus' name. Amen.

Personal Reflection:

_____

_____

_____

_____

_____

_____

_____

_____

_____

_____

_____

_____

_____

_____

_____

_____

_____

_____

_____

_____

_____

_____

FRIENDSHIP WITH GOD

Psalm 25:14
The LORD is a friend to those who fear him.
He teaches them his covenant.

Fear and *friendship*. Those words normally don't go together. How can the "friendship of the Lord" be for those who "fear him"? Doesn't fear cause us to run away? Isn't friendship for those who hang close?

Certainly, for some fear and friendship do not go together. Sin has created a gap between us and the Holy God. That gap of sin leaves us separated from God. God's final judgment on sin and sinners is forever. Man's sin problem produces fear, or certainly should!

However, God loves us so much that he did something to bridge the gap. He sent his Son, Jesus, to die on the cross for our sins. Jesus took the Father's judgment for our sins on himself. With Jesus, fear is our honor and respect for God, demonstrated by thankful obedience. Have you trusted in Jesus to make you a friend of God? If you haven't, I invite you to pray this prayer.

Dear God, I know right now that I am not your friend. My sin separates me from you. I know I can never bridge the gap between me and you, but right now I trust in your Son, Jesus Christ, who took my sins and died for them on the cross. I am asking that you make me your friend through the work of Jesus. In his name I pray. Amen.

Personal Reflection:

_____

_____

_____

_____

_____

_____

_____

_____

_____

_____

_____

_____

_____

_____

_____

_____

_____

_____

_____

_____

_____

_____

_____

MY FORTRESS

Psalm 27:1

The LORD is my light and my salvation—so why should I be afraid? The LORD is my fortress, protecting me from danger, so why should I tremble?

God finds me in the darkness, the place where fear of the unknown resides, but he doesn't leave me there. He is my personal light, revealing the sin of my heart, showing my desperate need, and illuminating the right path to take.

The Lord is my light! Why should I be afraid?

God seeks and saves those who are lost. I was wandering aimlessly through life, caught in the web of my sin. Then God rescued me. He forgave my sin, declared me "Not Guilty!" and clothed me with the righteousness of Jesus.

The Lord is my salvation! Why should I be afraid?

God surrounds me with his presence and protection. He gives me all the strength to do what he has called me to do. He never leaves me nor forsakes me. He is the rock to which I cling and the refuge to which I run.

The Lord is my fortress! Why should I tremble?

Father, you are my light! My salvation! My stronghold! You are on my side. There is no one and nothing to fear. In Jesus' name. Amen.

Personal Reflection:

_____

_____

_____

_____

_____

_____

_____

_____

_____

_____

_____

_____

_____

_____

_____

_____

_____

_____

_____

_____

_____

WAIT FOR THE LORD

Psalm 27:14
Wait patiently for the LORD. Be brave and courageous.
Yes, wait patiently for the LORD.

The fear of uncertainty causes us to run ... fast. We run to places we think will bring comfort. We run to places where the pain can be dulled, at least for a while. These are unhealthy places that deliver short-lived satisfaction and false hope.

God has a different prescription for uncertainty. He tells us to stay put. He calls us to wait for the confidence. When we feel like bolting, he says, "Be strong." When our courage is melting like hot wax, he says, "Take heart." Spurgeon wrote, "Wait at his door with prayer; wait at his foot with humility; wait at his table with service; wait at his window with expectancy."

Our waiting is not passing time for God to arrive from a distant place; he is always present with us. Our waiting is not to give God time to determine his plan of action. God is waiting for us to wait on him.

Father, it is so hard to wait. I like to take matters in my own hands.
Help me slow down and wait in prayer, in humility, in service,
and with expectancy. In Jesus' name. Amen.

Personal Reflection:

_____

_____

_____

_____

_____

_____

_____

_____

_____

_____

_____

_____

_____

_____

_____

_____

_____

_____

_____

_____

_____

MY SHIELD

Psalm 28:7
*The LORD is my strength and shield. I trust him with
all my heart. He helps me, and my heart is filled with joy.
I burst out in songs of thanksgiving.*

Ever feel like you don't measure up? Ever feel like life's assignment
is beyond your skill level? Convinced that you don't have what it
takes? Don't feel alone. The line of inadequacy stretches around the
block, but you don't have to stand stuck in the long line. Move out
of the line and find where your issue can be addressed.

In today's passage David readily admits he doesn't have what it
takes. If God didn't come to his aid, he concluded, "I will be like
those who go down to the pit" (Psalm 28:1 NIV). When God heard
his "cry for mercy," he broke out in the confession, "The LORD is
my strength" (NIV).

Real adequacy doesn't come from our winsome personality, framed
degrees hanging on our walls, or experience in our fields of expertise.
The long line of inadequacy is stacked with qualified people. The
ability to meet each challenge and opportunity of life must come
from the Lord. He is our strength and power. He is our shield of
protection. He is our source of trust. Help comes from him alone. Get
out of the line and acknowledge that your sufficiency is in the Lord.

*Father, we cannot do what you are calling us to do while stuck in
the long line of inadequacy. Give us the strength to move out
and find our sufficiency in you alone. In Jesus' name. Amen.*

Personal Reflection:

_____

_____

_____

_____

_____

_____

_____

_____

_____

_____

_____

_____

_____

_____

_____

_____

_____

_____

_____

_____

_____

_____

MY TIME IS IN YOUR HANDS

Psalm 31:14-15

But I am trusting you, O LORD, saying, "You are my God!"
My future is in your hands. Rescue me from those
who hunt me down relentlessly.

God is in complete control of all things. His sovereignty is not delegated or shared. He is intimately involved in the day-to-day affairs of my life. My days are in his hands.

All the days of my life are recorded in God's book "before one of them came to be" (Psalm 139:16 NIV). He knows where I will be and when I will be there. He knows when my last breath will be taken. My life will not be "cut short." My days are in his hands.

The fear of uncertainty flows from our limited images of God. Some picture him as a hand-wringing God who would like to help us, but isn't able. Others picture him as a weak God who would like to intervene, but can't. Many picture him as the "Great Clockmaker" who winds up history and lets time run its course. However, my God is worthy of my trust. All of my days are in his hands.

Father, I don't pretend to understand all the things that happen in my life, but I can say with the psalmist, "I am trusting you." I declare in faith that you are my God and my time is in your hands. In Jesus' name. Amen.

Personal Reflection:

_____

_____

_____

_____

_____

_____

_____

_____

_____

_____

_____

_____

_____

_____

_____

_____

_____

_____

_____

_____

_____

_____

_____

BE STRONG AND COURAGEOUS

Psalm 31:24

*So be strong and courageous, all you who put
your hope in the LORD!*

In the English language, "hope" is kind of a fuzzy word. It describes a wish or desire that something will happen or turn out a certain way. We might hope it doesn't rain tomorrow, but tomorrow brings a downpour. In our language hope has no guarantees.

In Scripture, "hope" is different. It designates a certainty, a definite. It pronounces a trust that what has been promised will come to pass. As believers we have an eternal hope. That doesn't mean we are optimistic that maybe if everything works out well we might spend eternity in heaven. The believer's hope is a certain confidence that is based on the work of Jesus; our eternity is with the Lord.

All you who have certain confidence that God loves you, that he sent his Son to pay the penalty of your sin, that the work of Jesus on the cross places you in a relationship with God, that the Holy Spirit lives within you to give you the strength you need to do what God has called you to do … demonstrate your confidence to the world. Be strong and courageous!

Father, thank you for the certainty of your person, presence, and power in our lives. Help us demonstrate to a watching world that our certain confidence is in you. In Jesus' name. Amen.

Personal Reflection:

_____

_____

_____

_____

_____

_____

_____

_____

_____

_____

_____

_____

_____

_____

_____

_____

_____

_____

_____

_____

_____

MY HIDING PLACE

Psalm 32:7

For you are my hiding place; you protect me from trouble.
You surround me with songs of victory.

When uncertainty comes, and it will, this psalm gives us three truths that we can drive like stakes into the ground to keep us steady. Let's consider each truth-stake.

You are my hiding place. When an EF5 tornado with winds reaching over 200 mph hit Moore, Oklahoma, people ran to a safe hiding place. When storms hit our lives, God is the hiding place we run to. In him there is safety and refuge.

You will protect me from trouble. Trouble will be no stranger to those walking on the earth. We live in a sinful world and will be impacted by the consequences. Trouble does not take the believer by surprise. Jesus said, "In this world you will have trouble. But take heart! I have overcome the world" (John 16:33 NIV). In Christ there is protection.

You surround me with songs of deliverance. Here David paints a powerful word picture of God's protection. As we stand in the middle of the storm, God surrounds us on all sides, above and below. He encircles and encases us with reminders that he is with us and will carry us through the storm.

When the fear of uncertainty rears its ugly head, drive it away with these three truths of God's safety, protection, and deliverance. He is the certainty in uncertain times.

Father, remind me of this verse when the fear of uncertainty begins to settle on my heart. Help me to fend off this fear with your safety, protection, and songs of deliverance. In Jesus' name. Amen.

Personal Reflection:

_____

_____

_____

_____

_____

_____

_____

_____

_____

_____

_____

_____

_____

_____

_____

_____

_____

THE LORD RESCUES THE BROKENHEARTED

Psalm 34:18
*The LORD is close to the brokenhearted; he rescues
those whose spirits are crushed.*

Broken hearts come in many forms. Some are caused by sixth grade breakups; others when a spouse walks out after 25 years. Some come from the rejection of a dear friend; others by reckless words that pierce like a sword. Broken hearts come from job loss, illness, loneliness, the deaths of loved ones, or the death of a dream.

Broken hearts come in many forms. Whatever the cause, here is something we know for sure: The Lord is right there with us! He never leaves or lets go of his children. He is close with his comfort. He rescues those who are crushed in spirit.

Here's the amazing thing: broken hearts highlight his presence. There is something about a crushed spirit that amplifies his voice. When our hearts hurt, we hear him more clearly and see him more plainly. Listen for his voice. He is close to you.

*Father, I pray for those who are reading this today with broken
hearts. Let them feel your presence. Let them sense your love.
Wrap your arms around them and let them be enveloped by
your closeness. In Jesus' name. Amen.*

Personal Reflection:

_____

_____

_____

_____

_____

_____

_____

_____

_____

_____

_____

_____

_____

_____

_____

_____

_____

_____

_____

_____

_____

_____

_____

GOD IS OUR REFUGE AND STRENGTH

Psalm 46:1-3

God is our refuge and strength, always ready to help in times of trouble. So we will not fear when earthquakes come and the mountains crumble into the sea. Let the oceans roar and foam. Let the mountains tremble as the waters surge!

Sometimes we experience an earthquake of the soul. Our world is shaken with the surges of uninvited waters. Waves of chaos pound our confused hearts. Yet when these inevitable times come, we can stand strong. Really?

The psalmist reminds us that when tough times come (and they will come), we always have God on our side. Like a fortified city secured by high, thick walls, God is our shelter of protection. Our security is not found in finances, armies, or physicians. God alone is our refuge and strength, and he is ever-present. People will come and go. Our God never leaves us.

Therefore, we will not fear! Spurgeon says it this way, "Evil may ferment, wrath may boil, and pride may foam, but the brave heart of holy confidence trembles not. Great men [and women] who are like mountains may quake for fear in times of great calamity, but the man [and woman] whose trust is in God needs never be dismayed."

Heavenly Father, I don't want to be fearful. I want to trust in you alone. Please draw me to yourself, to the safety of your person. Help me feel your strength and presence. Help me stand strong in you. In Jesus' name. Amen.

Personal Reflection:

_____

_____

_____

_____

_____

_____

_____

_____

_____

_____

_____

_____

_____

_____

_____

_____

_____

_____

_____

_____

_____

_____

STEADY HEARTS

Psalm 55:22
Give your burdens to the LORD, and he will take care of you.
He will not permit the godly to slip and fall.

Give your burdens to the Lord.

Don't gently carry them over and lay them down. Rear back and heave them like a fisherman throwing a big net into the sea. In fact, do this: write down your cares—your fear, anxiety, dread, doubt, turmoil, worry—on sheets of paper. Put them in a bag. Go to your church and cast the bag at the foot of the cross.

He will take care of you.

The Hebrew word translated "sustain" means "to support." God is there to keep your feet steady on the treacherous climbs. He is there to hold you up when you stumble. He contains the fear so it doesn't get out of control. He stands by your side at all times.

He will not permit the godly to slip and fall.

Life happens quickly and unexpectedly. Uninvited fear breaks down our doors with one phone call or test result, but when God is with us he will not let our faith fail. He will keep our hearts steady when the ground around us seems to be giving way.

Father, I throw my fears, dread, worry, and anxiety onto you. They are way too heavy for me. Please take them, discard them, and fill me with your peace. In Jesus' name. Amen.

Personal Reflection:

_____

_____

_____

_____

_____

_____

_____

_____

_____

_____

_____

_____

_____

_____

_____

_____

_____

_____

_____

_____

_____

IN GOD I TRUST

Psalm 56:3-4

But when I am afraid, I will put my trust in you. I praise God for what he has promised. I trust in God, so why should I be afraid? What can mere mortals do to me?

It is not a matter of "if I will ever be afraid" but "when." Note the first five words of today's passage. David, the man after God's own heart, was afraid. This psalm was written when the Philistines had overtaken him in Gath. Captured by the Philistines, now that would strike fear in the heart of any person.

However, when the waves of fear come crashing in, David chooses to trust. He moves his focus from the situation and locks in on God. Mere mortals may have seized him, but they cannot seize his God. For David, and for us, trusting God drives the fear away.

Who or what enemy has captured your heart? Use the natural fear as a warning signal. Let the rising tides of fear be held back by barricades of trust. Since God is with us, who can stand against us?

Father, when fear comes, it is so easy to be absorbed by the terror of the day and the "what ifs" of tomorrow. When we are afraid, help us put our trust and confidence in you. Replace our fear with faith. In Jesus' name. Amen.

Personal Reflection:

WAIT QUIETLY BEFORE HIM

Psalm 62:1-2

I wait quietly before God, for my victory comes from him.
He alone is my rock and my salvation, my fortress
where I will never be shaken.

Spiritually exhausted? Feel like you are chasing your tail? Busy, running hard, but getting nowhere fast? Could it be that you're spent from running hard after the wrong thing? Could it be that you are pretty much living your life for yourself? Could it be that your spiritual exhaustion is caused by the inward battle between your will and what God wills for you?

Today's passage explains where your weary soul can find rest. That escape from chasing your tail is found in God alone. In him, your eternity is set. He is the author and finisher of salvation. In him, you are secure. He is the Rock! In him, you are safe. He is an impenetrable fortress. Peace is found when we surrender our weary souls to him.

A person just sent me this quote from *The Time Keeper*: "Man alone measures time. Man alone chimes the hour. And, because of this, man alone suffers a paralyzing fear that no other creature endures. A fear of time running out." The best way to conquer this fear is to rest in the eternal One who transcends all time.

Heavenly Father, I am tired of running. I am tired of fearing that I will run out of time. Help me find my rest, peace, and calmness in you. Help me find security in the rock, and safety in the fortress so that I will not be shaken. In Jesus' name. Amen.

Personal Reflection:

_____

_____

_____

_____

_____

_____

_____

_____

_____

_____

_____

_____

_____

_____

_____

_____

_____

_____

_____

_____

_____

_____

HE'S HOLDING YOU

Psalm 63:8
I cling to you; your strong right hand holds me securely.

Sometimes all we can do is hold on. One doctor's visit leaves our minds spinning. One phone call changes the course of our days. One text leaves our hearts heavy. These are not the times when we feel like considering the five possible interpretations of a difficult passage. We may not be up for reading a book about the theology and practice of prayer. Sometimes all we can do is cling.

David wrote the words of today's passage when he was in a desert —a dry time, a lonely time. Maybe you can relate. Today you are in a desert of illness or loss, fear or doubt, confusion or anxiety. Your mind is swirling with questions about the future and real-time decisions. You are exhausted from the tests, the waiting, and the procedures. You are recouping from the treatments. You are reeling after the loss. Sometimes all you can do is cling.

You know what? That's all you need to do. Hold tight to the Father. Fasten yourself to him. The ride may be bumpy, so buckle up right next to him. His strong right hand is wrapped around you. He's clinging to you more tightly than you are clinging to him. He will never let you go. Wherever you are and whatever you're going through, keep clinging to the Father. That is the only place of real protection, encouragement, and peace.

Father, I am clinging to you! Thank you for holding tight to me.
Thank you for never letting me go. In Jesus' name. Amen.

Personal Reflection:

_____

_____

_____

_____

_____

_____

_____

_____

_____

_____

_____

_____

_____

_____

_____

_____

_____

_____

_____

_____

_____

FROM EVERLASTING TO EVERLASTING

Psalm 90:2
Before the mountains were born, before you gave birth to the earth and the world, from beginning to end, you are God.

God is eternal. There was never a time when he wasn't; there will never be a time when he ceases to exist. He has neither beginning nor end.

God is eternal. There is no succession of moments in his being. God never says, "My goodness, I don't know where April went." He is not on a 24-hour cycle of days, weeks, months, or years.

God is eternal. He sees all things equally vividly. As I write this, I am looking at my computer screen. In my peripheral vision, I can see my coffee mug, some books, a printer, and the hint of a beautiful spring day out my window. God sees all things from beginning to end at the same time, in living color!

God is eternal. While he sees all things equally vividly, God sees events in time and acts in time. He watches me throughout the day. In fact, he never takes his eyes off me. In every situation of my timed day, God gives me exactly what I need right when I need it.

God is eternal, and he loves me so much that he sent his Son to pay the penalty of my sins, so I can call him "Abba, Father." Amazing!

Eternal Father, I cannot comprehend your eternality, but I can experience your love and care. Thank you. In Jesus' name. Amen.

Personal Reflection:

_____

_____

_____

_____

_____

_____

_____

_____

_____

_____

_____

_____

_____

_____

_____

_____

_____

_____

_____

_____

_____

_____

UNFAILING LOVE

Psalm 94:18-19

I cried out, "I am slipping!" but your unfailing love, O LORD,
supported me. When doubts filled my mind, your comfort
gave me renewed hope and cheer.

Sometimes we can feel it coming on. Like a person who loses his footing on a steep climb, we can feel our emotions slipping. The waves of anxiety build until they crash into our hearts and drench our souls. Here it comes, the fear of uncertainty.

- Your boss wants to see you first thing in the morning.
- The doctor wants to run some more tests.
- Your mind swirls while you wait for news from the surgery.
- The doctor says, "I'm sorry. There is nothing more we can do."
- The savings are gone.
- He walks out the door.

Life is filled with things that cause uncertainty. The stuff of life is beyond our control, and it's the lack of control that causes our emotions to implode. What do we do when we are standing in the midst of life and feel the fear coming on? The psalmist instructs us to turn hard toward God.

It is our loving Father who comes to our aid. As we take on the crashing waves of uncertainty, he keeps us standing. When our feet begin to slip, he grabs us and holds on tight. His peace surpasses human understanding. His comfort brings joy even in the midst of stormy trials. When we know God as our Father, certain help is always present with us.

Father, some are reading this with hearts saturated by anxiety. Allow them right now to feel the calming comfort of your Spirit. Give them a certainty of your presence that always comes with a deep peace. Let them know that since you are for us, nothing can stand against us. In Jesus' name. Amen.

Personal Reflection:

_____

_____

_____

_____

_____

_____

_____

_____

_____

_____

_____

_____

_____

_____

_____

_____

GOD'S GREAT LOVE

Psalm 103:11

For his unfailing love toward those who fear him is as great as the height of the heavens above the earth.

God's love is something believers need to understand, accept, and apply. A. W. Tozer explains this attribute of God in his book, *The Knowledge of the Holy.*

God's love tells us that he is friendly and his Word assures us that he is our friend and wants us to be his friends. "No man with a trace of humility would first think that he is a friend of God; but the idea did not originate with men. God himself said that Abraham was his friend, and he desires the same friendship with us."

Love is an emotional identification. Tozer writes, "It is a strange and beautiful eccentricity of the free God that He has allowed His heart to be emotionally identified with men. Self-sufficient as He is, He wants our love and will not be satisfied till He gets it. Free as He is, He has let His heart be bound to us forever."

Love takes pleasure in its object. "The Lord," Tozer says, "takes peculiar pleasure in His saints ... Christ in His atonement has removed the bar to the divine fellowship. Now in Christ all believing souls are objects of God's delight."

Heavenly Father, thank you for loving me. Thank you for a relationship with you through Jesus. Thank you for calling me your friend. In Jesus' name. Amen.

Personal Reflection:

_____

_____

_____

_____

_____

_____

_____

_____

_____

_____

_____

_____

_____

_____

_____

_____

_____

_____

_____

_____

_____

_____

_____

LIMITLESS LOVE

Psalm 103:17-18

*But the love of the LORD remains forever with those who
fear him. His salvation extends to the children's children
of those who are faithful to his covenant, of those who
obey his commandments!*

"Love", says A. W. Tozer, "is an essential attribute of God." Tozer
explains that all of God's attributes are always at work together.
One is never held back in order to emphasize another. Let's think
about what that means for us.

God is self-existent, so his love has no beginning. There has never
been a time when God wasn't existent, so his love has always been
present. It is from everlasting.

God is eternal, so his love has no end. There will never be a time
when God ceases to exist, so his love will always be there. It is from
everlasting to everlasting.

God is infinite, so his love has no limits. There will never be a time
when God quits loving us. His love has no stopping point.

God is holy, so his love is pure. On our best day, man's love is
tainted by our sinfulness. By contrast, God's love and his motives
are completely pure. God's love for us is perfect.

I don't know what you are going through today, but I know this—
God loves you! He loves you with an everlasting love. God loves
you! He loves you with a limitless love. He will never stop loving
you. God loves you! His motivation in loving you is pure. He paid a
great price to redeem you from sin's slavery. You are accepted. You

are secure. You are significant. You are a child of the living God all because of his great love.

Father, thank you for your eternal, limitless, pure love. Help me to respond with a life of thanksgiving and honor demonstrated by obedience in all the areas of my life. In Jesus' name. Amen.

Personal Reflection:

_____

_____

_____

_____

_____

_____

_____

_____

_____

_____

_____

_____

_____

_____

_____

_____

HE WATCHES OVER YOU

Psalm 121:5-8

The LORD himself watches over you! The LORD stands beside you as your protective shade. The sun will not harm you by day, nor the moon at night. The LORD keeps you from all harm and watches over your life. The LORD keeps watch over you as you come and go, both now and forever.

The world is a shaky place in which to live. As I write this, the headlines say the Chinese have infiltrated a top U.S. weapons system. The attorney general of the U.S. possibly misled Congress. Wars continue around the world. The most shocking news of all—the Pittsburgh Pirates had their first winning season in 20 years!

Uncertainty is the only certainty. Things change in our lives from day to day. Tests, treatments, and surgeries are on this week's schedule for many reading this. Others have jobs that are on the brink. Too many marriages are hanging together with one last thin thread of commitment. However, there is one certainty in this uncertain world.

The unchanging God watches over you. He never sleeps, protecting you day and night. He leaves with you in the morning, comes home with you at night, and watches over you throughout the day. God is certain. He will hold you steady when your world seems like it's falling apart.

Father, help us hold on to you when the certain storm delivers uncertainty in our lives. In Jesus' name. Amen.

Personal Reflection:

_____

_____

_____

_____

_____

_____

_____

_____

_____

_____

_____

_____

_____

_____

_____

_____

_____

_____

_____

_____

_____

OMNIPRESENT

Psalm 139:7-10

I can never escape from your Spirit! I can never get away from your presence! If I go up to heaven, you are there; if I go down to the grave, you are there. If I ride the wings of the morning, if I dwell by the farthest oceans, even there your hand will guide me, and your strength will support me.

God is not limited by time or space. He is present everywhere at the same time in his whole being. There is nowhere in the entire universe, on land or sea, that a person can go and get away from God.

Admittedly, there are times when this is a disturbing truth. In our rebellion we want to escape God's presence. We don't want him around when we engage in sinful activities, but God doesn't play hide-and-seek. Wherever we go, he is already there.

Because of God's omnipresence, we are never alone. He is there in our laughter and our tears. He is there when we pump our fists with excitement and when we hang our heads in despair. He stands by our side as we watch our loved ones breathe their last. He walks with us from the grave and through our grief. He never leaves us nor forsakes us. The omnipresent God is Immanuel—God with us, through eternity.

Father, forgive us when we try to get away from you. Thank you for never leaving our side. In Jesus' name. Amen.

Personal Reflection:

FOREVER FAITHFUL

Psalm 146:3-6

Don't put your confidence in powerful people; there is no help for you there. When they breathe their last, they return to the earth, and all their plans die with them. But joyful are those who have the God of Israel as their helper, whose hope is in the LORD their God. He made heaven and earth, the sea, and everything in them. He keeps every promise forever.

What gives you confidence? What calms your heart? What makes you feel secure? A thriving economy? A secure job? Your person in the White House? A substantial retirement? A strong military?

Check out today's passage. Human beings, even the most powerful of them, cannot save. No person can deliver security. Death puts to rest any temptation to trust in man. On the day man dies, his ability to enact plans dies with him.

Therefore, put your trust in the One who remains faithful forever. He is the Maker of heaven, earth, the sea, and everything in them. Blessed is the person whose help and hope is in the Lord their God.

Father, it is tempting to put our trust in the stuff and people around us. Never let us forget that you are the only One who will stand with us throughout eternity. Thank you for remaining faithful forever. In Jesus' name. Amen.

Personal Reflection:

_____

_____

_____

_____

_____

_____

_____

_____

_____

_____

_____

_____

_____

_____

_____

_____

_____

_____

_____

_____

HE HEALS THE BROKENHEARTED

Psalm 147:3
He heals the brokenhearted and bandages their wounds.

God stands by the brokenhearted, but he doesn't just stand by. He is not a passive onlooker or a well-wisher. He doesn't need to go for help. He comes to us in our brokenness as the Divine Doctor, the Sovereign Surgeon, the Holy Healer. He brings exactly what we need at the precise moment we need it; not a moment too soon, not a second too late.

God stands by the brokenhearted. He comes to broken bodies and broken dreams. He arrives at the right time with the right prescription and injects us with the healing power of his Spirit. When he brings healing, confusion is driven away by calmness; panic is chased off by peace. He finds all the places where doubt has broken through and rebuilds the wall.

God stands by the brokenhearted. Difficult times can leave some painful places. We feel like God has left us and let us down. The "Why?" question is never far from our minds. Spiritual exhaustion is a close cousin to physical exhaustion. God comes to bind up our wounds. Don't hide your hurt. Tell him all about it. Tell him where it hurts. Uncover your wounds before God so he can gently bind them with his tender and caring touch.

Heavenly Father, thank you for standing by me in my brokenness. Thank you for binding my wounds. Help me uncover any wound I may be hiding. Thank you for your powerful work in my life. In Jesus' name. Amen.

Personal Reflection:

_____

_____

_____

_____

_____

_____

_____

_____

_____

_____

_____

_____

_____

_____

_____

_____

_____

_____

_____

_____

_____

_____

STRONG CONFIDENCE

Proverbs 14:26
*Those who fear the LORD are secure; he will be
a refuge for their children.*

The fear of the Lord is not a cowering terror or horror. It is the honor and respect of the heavenly Father demonstrated by doing what he says. A person's lip service does not equal an awe of God. It's one's obedience, even when no one else is looking, that confirms healthy fear.

A public or private prodigal will never experience confidence. Keeping our distance from God does not allow us to feel his embrace. Running away from God always leads to the land of discouragement, but the person who is following hard after Jesus will find a supernatural peace in his presence.

Others will benefit as well. Little eyes are watching your actions. Little hearts are feeling your emotions. Little feet are following. Only when our refuge is in the Lord will they have a genuine example of confidence.

Father, thank you for the promise of a life without fear; a life of strong confidence. Help us stay on your prescribed path for our sake and for the sake of our children. In Jesus' name. Amen.

Personal Reflection:

_____

_____

_____

_____

_____

_____

_____

_____

_____

_____

_____

_____

_____

_____

_____

_____

_____

_____

_____

_____

_____

THE STRONG FORTRESS

Proverbs 18:10-12

The name of the LORD is a strong fortress; the godly run to him and are safe. The rich think of their wealth as a strong defense; they imagine it to be a high wall of safety. Haughtiness goes before destruction; humility precedes honor.

Walls and towers were important parts of a biblical city's protection. Many cities built high towers at the corners of their walls. These towers were hollow with a staircase reaching to the top. Each one served as a watchtower to spot invading armies and provide the defensive upper hand. The height placed archers at a distinct advantage as the enemy approached.

Many people construct "strong defenses" today. Some are built with money. As our verse says, the rich imagine their wealth is "a high wall of safety." Others feel invincible due to their intelligence, expertise, training, or position; but pride in ourselves or in our stuff is always a red flag. Proverbs 18:12 reminds us that "Haughtiness goes before destruction."

Those who follow Jesus realize that only he is the place of security and protection. That's why we run to Jesus "and are safe." Only Christ protects us throughout this life. Jesus is the only One who can deliver us safely home.

Lord Jesus, thank you for being my strong fortress. Thank you for the invitation to come into your security throughout this life and throughout eternity. Amen.

Personal Reflection:

_____

_____

_____

_____

_____

_____

_____

_____

_____

_____

_____

_____

_____

_____

_____

_____

_____

_____

_____

_____

_____

_____

STEADFAST TRUST

Isaiah 26:3-4

You will keep in perfect peace all who trust in you, all whose thoughts are fixed on you! Trust in the LORD always, for the LORD GOD is the eternal Rock.

Satan comes with the "What if?" questions. "What if the surgery is not successful?" "What if the treatment doesn't work?" "What if the cancer returns?" "What if he leaves?" "What if the counseling doesn't work?" "What if he never comes back?" "What if my kids walk away from God?" Satan knows that questions fill our minds and hearts with chaos.

God comes with the invitation, "Trust!" Trust in the "eternal Rock" chases the chaos away. Trust replaces confusion and questions with a "perfect peace." Keeping our minds saturated with God keeps the waters calm even when the storm is raging all around us.

How do we keep our minds steadfast? Here are three suggestions:

1. Read God's Word. It is his love letter to you. Read through the Psalms and highlight his promises. There is calm under the shelter of his wings.

2. Listen to Christian music. Load your iPhone with music that reminds you of God's unconditional love. Soak in the words of the songs like you would soak in a hot bath. God uses music to soothe the soul.

3. Selectively speak with encouragers. Stay away from people who drag you down and turn your thoughts to doubting. Speak to friends who lift you with humor, care, and, most importantly, prayer.

Father, my mind can be easily distracted. One moment I feel my heart is full of faith, the next moment it is full of fear. Help me to keep my mind focused on you. You alone deliver the peace that passes human understanding. In Jesus' name. Amen.

Personal Reflection:

_____

_____

_____

_____

_____

_____

_____

_____

_____

_____

_____

_____

_____

_____

_____

_____

GOD'S ENDURING WORD

Isaiah 40:8
*"The grass withers and the flowers fade, but the word
of our God stands forever."*

Things change!

- Records became 8-track tapes that became cassettes that became CDs that became iTunes downloads.

- Computers took up large rooms then small rooms then desktops then laptops. Now they are held in your hand.

- Phones were in a booth on the corner then on the wall in your home then transported in a suitcase-sized carrier now easily fit in your pocket.

- Kids are born, grow up, go to college, get married, and move to another part of the country without asking your permission.

- The winter is pushed out by the spring then replaced by the summer then chased away by the fall. The grass dries up and the flowers fall off the stems.

Constant change is the only thing that doesn't change! Well, there is one other thing.

God's Word never changes. His promises are as certain today as they were when the ink of the inspired Word was still wet on the parchment. We can be sure that God's Word gives us instruction and promises that will never change or go out of style. That's why confidence and courage come from reading the Bible. It is an unshakable pillar for the heart.

Father, thank you for your enduring Word. Thank you for your unchanging promises. Help me find courage each day from your love letter to me. In Jesus' name. Amen.

Personal Reflection:

_____

_____

_____

_____

_____

_____

_____

_____

_____

_____

_____

_____

_____

_____

_____

_____

_____

_____

_____

THE SOVEREIGN LORD

Isaiah 40:10

Yes, the Sovereign LORD is coming in power. He will rule with a powerful arm. See, he brings his reward with him as he comes.

God's sovereignty is the attribute by which he rules over all creation. To be sovereign, God must be all-knowing, all-powerful, and absolutely free. A. W. Tozer explains the reasons for this in *The Knowledge of the Holy*.

All-knowing. If there were "one datum of knowledge, however small, unknown to God, His rule would break down at that point. To be Lord over all the creation, He must possess all knowledge."

All-powerful. If God were lacking "one infinitesimal modicum of power, that lack would end His reign and undo His kingdom; that one stray atom of power would belong to someone else and God would be a limited ruler and hence not sovereign."

Absolutely free. God must be "free to do whatever He wills to do anywhere at any time to carry out His eternal purpose in every single detail without interference. Were He less than free He must be less than sovereign."

In today's passage Isaiah tells us that God comes to us possessing great strength and bearing gifts. Think of it! The all-knowing, all-powerful, and absolutely free heavenly Father comes to you with a reward. Whatever your circumstance, you can trust him to bring good gifts to you. In fact, could it be that your situation, as difficult as it is, is a good gift in disguise?

Father, you are the sovereign LORD. We proclaim that you can be trusted! Give us the strength to trust. In Jesus' name. Amen.

Personal Reflection:

_____

_____

_____

_____

_____

_____

_____

_____

_____

_____

_____

_____

_____

_____

_____

_____

_____

_____

CLOSE TO HIS HEART

Isaiah 40:11

He will feed his flock like a shepherd. He will carry the lambs in his arms, holding them close to his heart. He will gently lead the mother sheep with their young.

The Good Shepherd cares for his sheep. He leads them where the grass is lush. He leads them to clear, fresh streams. He protects them from the animals that would attack and kill. He keeps his flock together. Not one sheep is ever lost. He leads purposefully and gently. Sometimes he picks up the weak ones and holds them in his arms. He carries them close to his heart so they can hear it beat.

Maybe today you feel weak in body. The procedures and treatments have drained your strength. Your energy is gone. Maybe you feel weak emotionally. Anxiety has overtaken your thoughts. Worry has worn you down. Perhaps you are spiritually weak. You have given in to temptation … again. You are frustrated by constant failure.

If you are exhausted in body, soul, and/or spirit, ask Jesus to gather you in his arms. Ask him to hold you close to his heart. Tell him you need to feel his presence and hear his heartbeat. His leadership is strong … and gentle. He will get you where you need to go, even if he has to carry you.

Father, I pray for those reading this who are worn out. Give them the assurance of your presence. Remind them of your love. Gather them in your arms and carry them close to your heart. Let them hear your heartbeat. Give them the strength they need to do what you are calling them to do. In Jesus' name. Amen.

Personal Reflection:

INCOMPREHENSIBLE

Isaiah 40:12-13

Who else has held the oceans in his hand? Who has measured off the heavens with his fingers? Who else knows the weight of the earth or has weighed the mountains and hills on a scale? Who is able to advise the Spirit of the LORD? Who knows enough to give him advice or teach him?

Someone has well said that we need to be reminded more than we need to be taught. I think there is a lot of truth to that. It is seldom a new nugget of truth that comforts me. More often it is the reminder of something I have forgotten, or at least pushed to a far corner of my heart.

It seems that Isaiah is following the "reminded more than taught" adage in today's passage. He doesn't provide new information but, by a series of rhetorical questions, he reminds us who God is.

> *Who else has held the oceans in his hand?*
> **Only God can do that!**
> *Or measured off the heavens with his fingers?*
> **That is a God thing for sure!**
> *Who else knows the weight of the earth?* **No one but God!**
> *Or weighed the mountains and hills on a scale?* **God!**
> *Who is able to advise the Spirit of the LORD?* **I certainly can't!**
> *Who knows enough to give him advice or teach him?* **No one!**

When you are in need of comfort and encouragement; when you need the courage to face another day, you don't need a new book. You need an old Book. Read God's Word to remind you who he is. Then ask the sovereign LORD to give you the strength you need.

Lord, as I read your Word, remind me again and again of who you are, who I am in you, and how much you love me. Never let me forget that I am a child of the sovereign LORD. In Jesus' name. Amen.

Personal Reflection:

_____

_____

_____

_____

_____

_____

_____

_____

_____

_____

_____

_____

_____

_____

_____

_____

THE SOURCE

Isaiah 40:14

Has the LORD ever needed anyone's advice? Does he need instruction about what is good? Did someone teach him what is right or show him the path of justice?

I am sitting here thinking how totally dependent I am. If some coffee grower somewhere in Guatemala hadn't done his job, I would have a serious headache right now. If some sardine fisherman slept in, I would have missed lunch. If some teenager had stayed at home, I would not be enjoying a diet vanilla Dr. Pepper from Sonic, and that's just for starters. From my clothes to my computer to the light in the room … I depend on others for my existence.

Not God. Our Creator doesn't rely on any being, person, or thing for his existence. He is the source of all things. He doesn't need instruction or counsel. He doesn't need a consultant or a teacher. He has owned all knowledge since eternity past. He is completely independent.

God's independence emboldens our trust. God's work is not slowed due to a shortage of natural resources. He is not waiting on a supplier. The economy does not impact his generosity. He has everything we need in and of himself, and he is not stingy with his blessings. Let him know what you need. He's got it.

Father, remind us often that you are independent and self-reliant.
May that knowledge help us trust you for all we need.
In Jesus' name. Amen.

Personal Reflection:

_____

_____

_____

_____

_____

_____

_____

_____

_____

_____

_____

_____

_____

_____

_____

_____

_____

_____

_____

_____

_____

_____

THE GREAT INVITATION
TO FEARLESSNESS

Isaiah 41:10
"Don't be afraid, for I am with you. Don't be discouraged,
for I am your God. I will strengthen you and help you.
I will hold you up with my victorious right hand."

God invites you to fearlessness. He invites you to walk away from your anxiousness. Yeah, I know it sounds a little crazy right now with all you are going through, but the One who makes the offer knows your situation inside and out. There is good reason to check "Accept."

The invitation to leave fear and anxiety is not based on you but on God, his presence and his person. He is with you right now in the middle of your circumstances, your questions, and your doubt. He is your God! You belong to him. He never takes his eyes off you.

He will give you everything you need for the journey ahead. He will provide you with the strength to face the challenges of every day and the fears of every night. He is at your side to help you through the steep paths and deep valleys. His strong right hand will never let you fall, whether you are walking in the daylight or stumbling in the dark. Let him carry your backpack of fear and anxiety. He is more than capable of handling the load.

Lord Jesus, our strength is depleted. Thank you for always holding us
up and never letting us fall. We admit that we are praising you one
minute and panicking the next. Thank you for never leaving us,
for giving us supernatural strength, and for walking with us through
our deepest joy and darkest night. Amen.

Personal Reflection:

_____

_____

_____

_____

_____

_____

_____

_____

_____

_____

_____

_____

_____

_____

_____

_____

_____

_____

_____

_____

_____

_____

_____

GOD'S PURPOSE WILL STAND

Isaiah 46:9-11

"Remember the things I have done in the past. For I alone am God! I am God, and there is none like me. Only I can tell you the future before it even happens. Everything I plan will come to pass, for I do whatever I wish. I will call a swift bird of prey from the east—a leader from a distant land to come and do my bidding. I have said what I would do, and I will do it."

- Regardless of terrorists' threats ...
  I alone am God! My purpose will stand.
- Regardless of the economic forecast ...
  I alone am God! My purpose will stand.
- Regardless of Supreme Court decisions ...
  I alone am God! My purpose will stand.
- Regardless of rogue rulers who make arrogant claims ...
  I alone am God! My purpose will stand.
- Regardless of nuclear buildups ...
  I am God, and there is no other. My purpose will stand.
- Even when the doctor's report is not what you wanted to hear ...
- Even when your spouse walks away ...
- Even when your dream dies ...
- Even when you don't get the job ...
- Even when your child is estranged ...
- Even when you are discouraged ...
- Even when grief hits you with a vicious uppercut ...
- Even when your heart is broken ...
- Even while you wait on God to answer ...

Remember God's promise: I alone am God! Everything I plan will come to pass.

Father, in our joy, sadness, disappointment, discouragement, confusion, and fear, we proclaim that you alone are God! Thank you that everything you plan will come to pass. In Jesus' name. Amen.

Personal Reflection:

_____

_____

_____

_____

_____

_____

_____

_____

_____

_____

_____

_____

_____

_____

_____

_____

_____

_____

IN HIS PRESENCE

Jeremiah 23:23-24

"Am I a God who is only close at hand?" says the LORD. "No, I am far away at the same time. Can anyone hide from me in a secret place? Am I not everywhere in all the heavens and earth?" says the LORD.

The message of Israel's false prophets was crafted to satisfy people rather than God. In response to Israel's sin, they offered an unfounded peace. False teachers from every generation bring messages their hearers desire to hear. To every deceitful teacher and prophet God says, in essence, "You've got to be kidding!"

In today's passage, God responds to the prophets by explaining two of his attributes. He is both omnipresent and omniscient. God is everywhere at the same time in his full being. He is both nearby and far away. God knows everything there is to know about everything there is to know! His knowledge and presence fill heaven and earth.

How can we apply these truths when we are fearful? First, wherever you are, God sees you. You are not hidden or alone. Second, whoever you are, God knows you. He knows you and your situation. He meets you right where you are, but he doesn't leave you there. He takes you to where he wants you to be.

Father, thank you for knowing where we are and who we are. Help us trust you when we are weak. Help us to have confidence when we are shaken. Replace our fears with your peace. In Jesus' name. Amen.

Personal Reflection:

GOD HAS GREAT PLANS FOR YOU

Jeremiah 29:11-13

"For I know the plans I have for you," says the LORD. "They are plans for good and not for disaster, to give you a future and a hope. In those days when you pray, I will listen. If you look for me wholeheartedly, you will find me."

Whatever your circumstance, I can promise you this: God has not forgotten you and he will not forsake you. Even if it seems like you're alone, you are not. Even when it seems like God has removed his blessings from you, he has not.

The powerful promise in today's passage was written to exiles! King Nebuchadnezzar overthrew Jerusalem, ransacked the city, and carried the survivors off to Babylon. Jeremiah wrote these words to people living away from their homeland and family, feeling helpless. The prophet reminded them that God had not forgotten them.

You may feel exiled from God today, carried off to your "Babylon" of illness, separation, discouragement, grief, or rejection. Remember, God will never leave you. His plans for you involve hope and a future! When you pray, he will listen. When you seek him, you will find him. When God is our Father, our best days are always ahead.

Father, thank you for this great promise! Remind us today that the plans for your children are always good. Thank you for sending your Son to give us a certain hope and an eternal future. Thank you for listening when we pray. Help us seek you with all our hearts. In Jesus' name. Amen.

Personal Reflection:

_____

_____

_____

_____

_____

_____

_____

_____

_____

_____

_____

_____

_____

_____

_____

_____

_____

_____

_____

_____

_____

_____

_____

NOTHING IS TOO HARD FOR YOU

Jeremiah 32:17

"O Sovereign LORD! You made the heavens and earth by your strong hand and powerful arm. Nothing is too hard for you!"

God is all-powerful. He is able to do anything and everything consistent with his will. Nothing is too hard for him. God specializes in the impossible.

God's power is infinite. He is not limited to do only the things he has already done. He is able to do more than he actually does. John the Baptist said that God could raise stones to become children of Abraham if he so chose (Matthew 3:9). God "does as he wishes" (Psalm 115:3). The angel told Mary, "For the word of God will never fail" (Luke 1:37). Jesus said, "With God everything is possible" (Matthew 19:26).

Do you believe that? Yeah, I know your situation may seem absolutely impossible. You are up against the wall, at the end of your rope. You feel helpless and hopeless, but that's when God does his best work. The apostle Paul said that God is "able, through his mighty power at work within us, to accomplish infinitely more than we might ask or think" (Ephesians 3:20). Trust in him as the omnipotent God.

*Father, I pray for the person in a seemingly impossible situation.
I pray that you will work in their heart and their situation. Show
them that you are the One who specializes in impossible situations.
In Jesus' name. Amen.*

Personal Reflection:

_____

_____

_____

_____

_____

_____

_____

_____

_____

_____

_____

_____

_____

_____

_____

_____

_____

_____

_____

_____

_____

_____

_____

ABLE TO DELIVER

Daniel 3:17-18

"If we are thrown into the blazing furnace, the God whom we serve is able to save us. He will rescue us from your power, Your Majesty. But even if he doesn't, we want to make it clear to you, Your Majesty, that we will never serve your gods or worship the gold statue you have set up."

The Babylonian king, Nebuchadnezzar, overthrew Judah and took the best and brightest back to Babylon. Among the young men he took captive were Shadrach, Meshach, and Abednego. When the captives were ordered to bow down and worship an image of gold, these three Israelites refused and were sentenced to a blazing furnace; but they lived without fear.

The three were confident that God was able to deliver them. Even if God did not see fit to deliver them from the fire, they remained unfazed. "We want to make it clear to you, Your Majesty, that we will never serve your gods or worship the gold statue ..." With the furnace heated seven times hotter than normal, the three young men were thrown into the fire. When Nebuchadnezzar looked into the flames, the three were unharmed because God had sent an angel to protect them.

Living without fear is the confidence that God can deliver us from anything at any time. However, even if he chooses to let us perish in the fire, we will still refuse to bow down before anyone or anything but him. Living without fear is the confidence of knowing that our life, death, and eternity are in his hands.

Father, we belong to you. Help us obey you and honor you even when the battle continues, and even when we walk through the fire. May we submit our will to yours and trust you to deliver us safely home. In Jesus' name. Amen.

Personal Reflection:

_____

_____

_____

_____

_____

_____

_____

_____

_____

_____

_____

_____

_____

_____

_____

_____

_____

FEARLESS

Daniel 6:10-11

But when Daniel learned that the law had been signed, he went home and knelt down as usual in his upstairs room, with its windows open toward Jerusalem. He prayed three times a day, just as he had always done, giving thanks to his God. Then the officials went together to Daniel's house and found him praying and asking for God's help.

Like Shadrach, Meshach, and Abednego, Daniel was in the group taken captive to Babylon. When a decree went out that the king was the only person to be prayed to, Daniel ignored the command. He went home and prayed to God before open windows. He would not deny his Lord.

Daniel's obedience resulted in a death sentence. He was thrown into a den of lions, but God sent his angel and shut the mouths of the hungry beasts. When Daniel was lifted from the pit, "not a scratch was found on him, for he had trusted in his God" (Daniel 6:23).

Living without fear is living a life of trust. Our lives will be filled with inevitable challenges. How we handle the challenges is the issue. Fear causes us to freeze or run to unhealthy places. Trust allows us to follow God wherever the path leads … even to a lions' den. Even there in the pit, we will find that God is more than enough. Whatever your "lions' den," trust God. He will deliver you from the pit.

Father, I need your help to trust you. Too often, fear overtakes my soul. Protect me from my propensity to freeze or run away. Fill me with your confidence and drive the fear from my heart. In Jesus' name. Amen.

Personal Reflection:

_____

_____

_____

_____

_____

_____

_____

_____

_____

_____

_____

_____

_____

_____

_____

_____

_____

_____

_____

_____

_____

THE LORD CARES FOR YOU

Nahum 1:7
The LORD is good, a strong refuge when trouble comes.
He is close to those who trust in him.

The Lord is good. God always has our best interests at heart. He never wastes our time. He is working in you today to prepare you for tomorrow. His assignments are not always easy. In fact, sometimes they are very hard, but he never leaves nor forsakes us. He has great plans for our future.

The Lord is a refuge in times of trouble. Jesus reminded us that in this life we will have trouble. Challenges will shake our faith. Questions will fill our hearts. Sometimes doubts will sprout up. These are normal responses. In challenging times, God is always our shelter and protection. Run to his open arms and feel his strong embrace.

The Lord is close to those who trust in him. Religions of the world have a god who doesn't care. Man must work hard to get the god's attention. Man must somehow prove his worth. However, the Bible teaches us the amazing truth that God came to man. He loves us so much that he sent his Son. Since he loves us so much that he sent Jesus to take care of our eternity, we can be confident that he cares for us today. He can always be trusted.

Father, today is a difficult day. Remind me by your Spirit that lives in me that you are good, that you are my shelter, and that you care for me. I need that reassurance today. I am listening for your voice. In Jesus' name. Amen.

Personal Reflection:

_____

_____

_____

_____

_____

_____

_____

_____

_____

_____

_____

_____

_____

_____

_____

_____

_____

_____

_____

_____

_____

THE SOVEREIGN LORD IS MY STRENGTH

Habakkuk 3:17-19

Even though the fig trees have no blossoms, and there are no grapes on the vines, even though the olive crop fails, and the fields lie empty and barren; even though the flocks die in the fields, and the cattle barns are empty, yet I will rejoice in the LORD! I will be joyful in the God of my salvation! The Sovereign LORD is my strength! He makes me as surefooted as a deer, able to tread upon the heights.

Strength is not found in stuff. In fact, there are times when the stuff just isn't there. Inadequacy may be the reality, but fear doesn't have to be the result.

Today's passage is one of my favorites. It shoots down the prosperity teaching that promises tenfold material return on my giving. Sometimes the fig tree does not bud, vines are fruitless, crops fail, pens and stalls are empty. That's reality, isn't it? However, there's another reality. Even when I am going through a tough stretch, "yet I [can] rejoice in the LORD! I [can] be joyful in the God of my salvation!"

The fear of inadequacy is met when I realize that "the Sovereign Lord is my strength." In the face of an impossible situation, an impasse, God enables me to "tread upon the heights." God gives me all I need to climb my personal pole of fear. With God on my side, I don't have to fear fruitless vines, empty stalls, or cropless fields. God plus nothing else is more than enough to quench my fears.

Father, drive this truth deep into my fearful heart.
Help me keep my trust settled in you alone. In Jesus' name. Amen.

Personal Reflection:

_____

_____

_____

_____

_____

_____

_____

_____

_____

_____

_____

_____

_____

_____

_____

_____

_____

_____

_____

MIGHTY TO SAVE!

Zephaniah 3:17

"For the LORD your God is living among you. He is a mighty savior. He will take delight in you with gladness. With his love, he will calm all your fears. He will rejoice over you with joyful songs."

Whatever you are going through today, God is on your side. We are always held by the embrace of his presence, strength, and love. Today's verse, tucked away in the Old Testament, is a great reminder of who God is and how he works in our lives. Let's consider the truths of this passage one at a time.

The LORD your God is living among you. The eternal God is always with us. In our great joy or deep sorrow, he is there. He provides comfort, encouragement, instruction, correction, and strength. He never leaves nor forsakes us.

He is a mighty savior. There is nothing in our lives that is too big for God. He will give us all we need to do everything he calls us to do.

He will take delight in you with gladness. God sent Jesus to die just for you! That's how much he loves you! You are a child of the living God. He takes great pleasure in you.

With his love, he will calm all your fears. Life has a way of cranking up the anxiety level. Things come into our lives that cause stress and doubt, but that's when the Holy Spirit takes over. He breathes calmness into our souls. He reminds us that he is on our side.

He will rejoice over you with joyful songs. We know what it's like to sing songs to God, but do you realize the heavenly Father sings over us? Like a father and mother sing to their children, God sings songs of joy over us. That amazes me!

Heavenly Father, thank you for never leaving me alone. Thank you for your power to save me from my sins and myself. Thank you for taking pleasure in me. Thank you for calming my anxious heart. Thank you for rejoicing over me. Thank you for being my heavenly Father. In Jesus' name. Amen.

Personal Reflection:

UNCHANGEABLE

Malachi 3:6
"I am the LORD, and I do not change. That is why you descendants of Jacob are not already destroyed."

Everything changes. Money comes and goes. Investments are up and down. Spring becomes summer becomes fall becomes winter. Kids mature. Adults age. There are changes in jobs, homes, cities, and lifestyles. Everything changes.

God is immutable. Although God acts and feels emotions, he is unchanging in his being, perfection, and promises. The Dutch theologian Herman Bavinck notes the great significance of this attribute:

The doctrine of God's immutability is of the highest significance for religion. The contrast between being and becoming marks the difference between the creator and the creature. Every creature is continually becoming. It is changeable, constantly striving, seeks rest and satisfaction, and finds this rest in God, in him alone, for only he is pure being and no becoming.[1]

Find rest today in God's immutability. He is "pure being and no becoming." He is the Rock. He doesn't change like shifting shadows (James 1:17). He is the same yesterday, today, and forever (Hebrews 13:8). He will not change his mind, his position, or his promises. Let your fearful heart settle peacefully on the unchanging and unchangeable person of God.

---

[1] Wayne Gruden, *Systematic Theology*, 163–164.

Father, thank you for being our Rock. Thank you for the certainty and security of your immutability. Thank you for never renegotiating your promises to us even when we renege on our promises to you. In Jesus' name. Amen.

Personal Reflection:

_____

_____

_____

_____

_____

_____

_____

_____

_____

_____

_____

_____

_____

_____

_____

_____

_____

_____

FINDING REST

Matthew 11:28
Then Jesus said, "Come to me, all of you who are weary and carry heavy burdens, and I will give you rest."

Jesus' special invitation is for all who are carrying heavy loads. The weight wears a person down mentally, physically, and spiritually. There is only one remedy for body and soul exhaustion—rest. And that's exactly what Jesus promises.

You have never received an invitation like this! Jesus himself requests your presence. He wants you to come to him. He doesn't like distance. He has something to give you that you can't find anywhere else. He is motioning for you. Don't hesitate. He will give you rest!

This verse reminds me of Hillsong's "Forever Reign." The second verse and chorus go like this:

You are peace, You are peace / When my fear is crippling / You are true, You are true / Even in my wandering / You are joy, You are joy / You're the reason that I sing / You are life, You are life, / In You death has lost its sting

Here's the chorus. Let this be your prayer:

Oh, I'm running to Your arms, / I'm running to Your arms / The riches of Your love / Will always be enough / Nothing compares to Your embrace / Light of the world forever reign

Personal Reflection:

_____

_____

_____

_____

_____

_____

_____

_____

_____

_____

_____

_____

_____

_____

_____

_____

_____

_____

_____

_____

_____

UNFAILING FAITH

Luke 22:31-34

"Simon, Simon, Satan has asked to sift each of you like wheat. But I have pleaded in prayer for you, Simon, that your faith should not fail. So when you have repented and turned to me again, strengthen your brothers." Peter said, "Lord, I am ready to go to prison with you, and even to die with you." But Jesus said, "Peter, let me tell you something. Before the rooster crows tomorrow morning, you will deny three times that you even know me."

In his classic work, *The Screwtape Letters*, C. S. Lewis wrote,

> *There are two equal and opposite errors into which our race can fall about the devils. One is to disbelieve in their existence. The other is to believe, and to feel an excessive and unhealthy interest in them. They themselves are equally pleased by both errors and hail a materialist or a magician with the same delight.*

Certainly an "excessive and unhealthy interest" in the demonic realm is dangerous, but, as Lewis reminds us, so is disbelieving or ignoring their existence. Satan is real. He prowls around like a roaring lion. He desires that we fail. He also desires that we are afraid of failing.

Notice that Jesus didn't pray that Peter would not fail. In fact, he said that the leader of the disciples would deny him three times. Jesus prayed that Peter's faith would not fail. Failure will visit us from time to time as we travel the human trail. But when we fail, our faith doesn't have to. Jesus is praying for us just like he prayed for Peter.

Lord Jesus, thank you for praying for us. When we stumble and fall, keep our faith strong so that we can turn back to your path and strengthen others. Amen.

Personal Reflection:

_____

_____

_____

_____

_____

_____

_____

_____

_____

_____

_____

_____

_____

_____

_____

_____

A CHILD OF GOD

John 1:12-13

But to all who believed him and accepted him, he gave the right to become children of God. They are reborn—not with a physical birth resulting from human passion or plan, but a birth that comes from God.

In his song "Identity," Lecrae raps, "I'm not the shoes I wear. I'm not the clothes I buy. I'm not the house I live in. I'm not the cars I drive, no. I'm not the job I work. You can't define my worth by nothing on God's green earth. My identity is found in Christ, is found in Christ." You may or may not appreciate Christian rap, but you can't deny the biblical truth found in this song.

Too many people—yes, even believers—find their significance in stuff. I feel better about myself when I am wearing the "right" clothes. I hold my head higher when I write the "right" address. Check out how significant I really am when you see me driving "the car." When I share my vocation at a dinner party and the prestige that comes with it, then I really feel significant.

When my identity is found in what I wear, where I live, what I drive, or what I do, I am plagued by an internal fear of insignificance. These things don't last. Significance comes only when my identity is in Christ. Nothing can change that. It never goes out of style. It never rusts or decays. It never gets old or breaks down. I am a child of God and will forever be!

Father, please don't let me look for significance in possessions, position, or appearance. Remind me often that I am your child and will be your child forever. In Jesus' name. Amen.

Personal Reflection:

_____
_____
_____
_____
_____
_____
_____
_____
_____
_____
_____
_____
_____
_____
_____
_____
_____
_____
_____
_____
_____
_____

CONFIDENCE IN DEATH

John 3:16

"For this is how God loved the world: He gave his one and only Son, so that everyone who believes in him will not perish but have eternal life."

The ending starts at the beginning. At birth the body, always vulnerable to a disease or tragic demise, begins the process of aging, which culminates in a worn-out, weakened fight for the last breath. Death is the feared and final enemy (1 Corinthians 15:26).

However, it doesn't have to be. God provided a way for death to transition us to life. We are sinners deserving eternal death—separation from God forever. Now that is something to fear! But God loved us so much that he sent his Son to pay sin's penalty on the cross. Jesus died so that we could live—forever!

The transition is personally put into effect when I believe in Jesus alone as the One who paid the penalty for my sins. When I trust in the work of Jesus on my behalf, spiritual death is replaced with a spiritual heartbeat. Physical death is simply a transition, and eternal death is replaced with eternal life. Because of Jesus, I can know with certainty that when I die I will pass from physical death to everlasting life! That's confidence!

Dear heavenly Father, thank you for sending Jesus to die on the cross for my sins. Thank you that I can live with confidence, knowing that when I close my eyes in death, I will open them to see my Savior. In Jesus' name. Amen.

Personal Reflection:

FROM DEATH TO LIFE

John 5:24

"I tell you the truth, those who listen to my message and believe in God who sent me have eternal life. They will never be condemned for their sins, but they have already passed from death into life."

There are many reasons you may have for not being a Christian. You may not feel like you need Jesus. You may not believe the Bible to be true. You may have had a bad experience with a church or with Christians. However, there is one thing that we can all agree on—we are going to die.

The obituary section of your local newspaper is filled with people whose lives on earth have come to an end. Some were great achievers while others lived a fairly common life. Some were old, others were young. Some died suddenly, others suffered from a long illness. One day your name and mine will be in the obituary section of the newspaper, but … what then?

You don't have to live in fear of death. The Bible is clear that you can cross over from death to eternal life. God sent his Son to make that crossing possible. Our sins separate us from God, so Jesus came to die for our sins. When we trust in his work on the cross, we will not be judged because he bore our sins in his body on the cross. He was judged for us. Have you trusted in Jesus to carry you from death to life? Would you like to? Then use this prayer as a guide to tell Jesus your heart's desire:

Dear Jesus, I am scared to die. I am scared of the unknown, but mainly I am scared because I don't know where I will spend eternity. I want to change that. You bore my sins in your body and died for them. You were judged for my sin so that I wouldn't have to be. Today I trust in you and your work for me on the cross. I trust you to carry me from death to eternal life. My trust is in you alone. Amen.

Personal Reflection:

_____

_____

_____

_____

_____

_____

_____

_____

_____

_____

_____

_____

_____

_____

_____

_____

_____

RESURRECTION!

Jesus told her, "I am the resurrection and the life. Anyone who believes in me will live, even after dying. Everyone who lives in me and believes in me will never ever die. Do you believe this, Martha?"

Jesus' words in today's passage were spoken to a woman in despair. Her brother, Lazarus, had died, and she felt the sharp pains of grief; but Jesus reminded her that while physical death was inevitable, spiritual death was not. Those who believe in Jesus "will never ever die."

After speaking these words, Jesus proved that he was indeed the resurrection and the life. He stood in front of the dead man's tomb and called him from the grave. Lazarus came out still in his grave clothes. This miracle showed what happens in the death of every believer. Jesus calls those who know him from death to life.

Jesus is the resurrection and the life. Whoever believes in him as the only way to God has the assurance of resurrection. The story of Lazarus was not the experience of one man, but the certain future of all who know Jesus as their personal Savior. Those who believe in Jesus will never die!

Heavenly Father, the unknown path of death brings fear. We see darkness, pain, weakness, separation, and then … then what? Remind us today of your great promise. Burn into our hearts the truth that those who know Jesus will live even though the body fails. Like Lazarus, Jesus will call us from death to life. In his name. Amen.

Personal Reflection:

_____

_____

_____

_____

_____

_____

_____

_____

_____

_____

_____

_____

_____

_____

_____

_____

_____

_____

_____

_____

WITH JESUS FOREVER

John 14:1-3

"Don't let your hearts be troubled. Trust in God, and trust also in me. There is more than enough room in my Father's home. If this were not so, would I have told you that I am going to prepare a place for you? When everything is ready, I will come and get you, so that you will always be with me where I am."

Heaven is real existence. Heaven is not a state of mind. Jesus told his disciples that he was going to get it ready. He promised he would come and take his followers to be with him. We will not float forever in a mental neverland. Heaven is for real.

Heaven is a real place. Jesus said, "I am going to prepare a place for you." He described heaven in our terminology, a house with many rooms. Later, John would try to describe its incomparable magnificence and beauty in the Revelation. Heaven is for real.

Heaven is for real believers. Jesus spoke the words in today's passage to his disciples, those who believed in him as the Son of God and trusted in his work on the cross as the only way to have a relationship with God. When they asked how to get to heaven, Jesus said, "I am the way, the truth, and the life. No one can come to the Father except through me." (John 14:6). Our confidence and certainty is found only in the person of Jesus. The path to forever is paved by the work of Christ.

Father, thank you for allowing us to know that we belong to Jesus and will spend eternity in heaven. We don't have to guess or wish or hope that one day we might go to heaven. Thank you that we can know for sure. In this life nothing else really matters. In Jesus' name. Amen.

Personal Reflection:

_____

_____

_____

_____

_____

_____

_____

_____

_____

_____

_____

_____

_____

_____

_____

_____

_____

_____

_____

_____

_____

CONNECTED

John 15:5

"Yes, I am the vine; you are the branches. Those who remain in me, and I in them, will produce much fruit. For apart from me you can do nothing."

After a windy day, dead branches lay all over our yard. Dead branches are, well, dead. No leaves; no life. We either throw them away or put them on top of our firewood to be used for kindling. Okay, Lori either throws them away or puts them on top of the firewood.

Have you ever felt like a dead branch? Not good for much? Not very effective? Not up for the task? The feeling of inadequacy can paralyze us to the point of uselessness, frozen in our fear of insufficiency. However, with Jesus *inadequacy* is a word that never applies.

Jesus is the life-giving vine. We are the living branches. To be sure, apart from him we are like dead branches; we "can do nothing." When we are connected to the source, we are alive! We are always up for the task! We are always effective! We will bear much fruit! Stay connected to Christ, and the fear of inadequacy is driven away by the fruit of sufficiency. Jesus takes our failures and our fears, and he infuses them with lasting life.

Lord Jesus, apart from you, fear reigns. Keep us connected and remaining in you, so we can leave our lives of fear and thrive with lives of fruitfulness. Amen.

Personal Reflection:

_____

_____

_____

_____

_____

_____

_____

_____

_____

_____

_____

_____

_____

_____

_____

_____

_____

_____

_____

_____

_____

_____

_____

_____

GRACE AND POWER

Acts 7:59-60

As they stoned him, Stephen prayed, "Lord Jesus, receive my spirit." He fell to his knees, shouting, "Lord, don't charge them with this sin!" And with that, he died.

Stephen was a man "full of God's grace and power" who did "amazing miracles and signs among the people" (Acts 6:8). When opposition came against the early Christians, he was one of the first to be arrested. As he faced the accusers during his trial, all who saw him said "his face became as bright as an angel's" (Acts 6:15).

For his defense, Stephen preached a powerful sermon proving from Scripture that Jesus was the long-awaited Messiah, but the Jews weren't buying it. They dragged him out of the city and began to stone him. Amazingly, even as the rocks were killing him, he asked God not to hold this sin against those putting him to death. Then he died.

Living without fear allows us to face death without fear. We have the confidence, based on God's Word, that we will pass from death to life, that we will fall asleep in the Lord. Death is the last dreaded enemy, but living without fear allows us to die without fear. Our trust in life and death is in Christ alone.

Lord Jesus, thank you for the confidence of knowing that we will pass from death to life. Thank you for meeting us in death and taking us home. In your name we pray. Amen.

Personal Reflection:

_____

_____

_____

_____

_____

_____

_____

_____

_____

_____

_____

_____

_____

_____

_____

_____

_____

_____

_____

_____

_____

_____

NOT GUILTY!

Romans 5:1

Therefore, since we have been made right in God's sight by faith, we have peace with God because of what Jesus Christ our Lord has done for us.

The fear of insignificance arises when we compare ourselves to the standard of the world. However, when we realize that we have "peace with God because of what Jesus Christ our Lord has done for us," that should change everything.

All believers have been "justified"! That rich theological word is one we need to understand in order to grasp our significance. "Justify" is a legal term that carries two significant truths.

- **"Not Guilty!"** As a sinner I stand before God without a prayer. I am guilty to the core but, thankfully, I don't have to stand before God alone. When I place my faith in Jesus and his work on the cross, he stands with me. Jesus died for all my sin and guilt. With Jesus, God pronounces me "not guilty." The payment for my sin has been settled in full by my Savior.

- **"Righteous!"** As I stand before God with Jesus, I am declared innocent and righteous. The word "righteous" is a term that comes from a river reed that was used as a construction tool to judge the horizontal straightness of walls and fences. The word is used in Scripture to describe God. He is the straight edge (the right rule) by which all things are evaluated. Because of Jesus, God clothes us with a "robe of righteousness" (Isaiah 61:10).

I am not significant because of who I am or what I do for a living. The name or address on my mailbox does not make me important. My significance is found in Jesus alone.

Lord Jesus, thank you for doing for me what I could never do for myself. Thank you for paying sin's penalty on my behalf. Lord, thank you for allowing me to find my identity in you alone. Amen.

Personal Reflection:

_____

_____

_____

_____

_____

_____

_____

_____

_____

_____

_____

_____

_____

_____

_____

WHEN YOU CAN'T PRAY

Romans 8:26-27

And the Holy Spirit helps us in our weakness. For example, we don't know what God wants us to pray for. But the Holy Spirit prays for us with groanings that cannot be expressed in words. And the Father who knows all hearts knows what the Spirit is saying, for the Spirit pleads for us believers in harmony with God's own will.

There are times when words won't come. We have said all we know to say every way we know to say it. We are not giving up or giving up on God. We are desperate for his help and strength. We are simply exhausted from wrestling in prayer. Can you relate?

God knows there will be times when we are worn out, but look at today's passage. When we are done, the Holy Spirit is just beginning! He takes over in our weakness. When words won't come, the Spirit prays on our behalf with deep groanings that cannot be translated into human words. This is not "speaking in tongues." This is God the Spirit praying for us to God the Father through our intercessor, God the Son.

God knows our weaknesses and he is there to help us. He will never leave us alone. He will not stand silently by in our suffering. The Holy Spirit is praying for you as you pray and when you are prayed out. Best of all, he is praying for you according to God's perfect will.

Holy Spirit, thank you for praying for me when I can't. Thank you for praying for me deeply and meaningfully. Thank you for praying for me in line with God's perfect will. In Jesus' name. Amen.

Personal Reflection:

_____

_____

_____

_____

_____

_____

_____

_____

_____

_____

_____

_____

_____

_____

_____

_____

_____

_____

_____

_____

_____

_____

SECURE!

Romans 8:38-39

And I am convinced that nothing can ever separate us from God's love. Neither death nor life, neither angels nor demons, neither our fears for today nor our worries about tomorrow—not even the powers of hell can separate us from God's love. No power in the sky above or in the earth below—indeed, nothing in all creation will ever be able to separate us from the love of God that is revealed in Christ Jesus our Lord.

I grew up believing that I could lose my relationship with God. I thought that I could be a Christian in the morning, sin at lunch, and be headed for hell in the afternoon. I thought that my relationship with Jesus depended on me. How about you? What does your relationship with God depend on?

One day as I was studying Scripture, I learned the truth found in today's passage. God has promised that nothing can separate me from his love found in Christ alone. It was like a burden had been lifted from my shoulders. That day, standing on a hot parking lot in Dallas, Texas, I learned that I was a child of God and would forever be.

Nothing in all creation can separate me from the love of God, not even death. That means that after death God still loves me. That means that after death I am aware of his love. That means that after death I am still alive! For the believer, death is simply a transition from the love of God on earth to the love of God in heaven, forever.

Dear Father, I stand firm in the truth that nothing can separate me from you. I know that no power in heaven or earth can remove me from your love. Today I stand secure in Jesus. In his name I pray. Amen.

Personal Reflection:

_____

_____

_____

_____

_____

_____

_____

_____

_____

_____

_____

_____

_____

_____

_____

_____

_____

_____

_____

_____

_____

_____

_____

THE MAGNITUDE OF GOD

Romans 11:33-36

Oh, how great are God's riches and wisdom and knowledge! How impossible it is for us to understand his decisions and his ways! For who can know the LORD's thoughts? Who knows enough to give him advice? And who has given him so much that he needs to pay it back? For everything comes from him and exists by his power and is intended for his glory. All glory to him forever! Amen.

Freedom from fear is not found in a person or possessions. It is found in God alone. Fear is driven away when we understand the magnitude of God. Included in this passage are seven truths about God's greatness.

1. ***God is beyond man's full discovery.*** On our best day with our clearest thinking, we will never be able to fully ascertain "how great are God's riches and wisdom and knowledge."

2. ***God's ways are beyond man's comprehension.*** There is no way our finite minds can grasp the infinite Creator.

3. ***God is beyond the need for man's counsel.*** God does not need man's advice on how to run the universe.

4. ***God is not indebted to man.*** No man offered anything to God that he needs to repay.

5. ***God is the first cause.*** He is the source from which all things come.

6. ***God is the efficient cause.*** He is the agent through which all things exist.

7. ***God is the final cause.*** To him all things return and await his judgment.

When we begin to understand the enormity of God, the One we know personally through Jesus, there is no room for fear.

Father, help our understanding of your person and fill our hearts with your peace. In Jesus' name. Amen

Personal Reflection:

_____

_____

_____

_____

_____

_____

_____

_____

_____

_____

_____

_____

_____

_____

_____

_____

_____

GOD'S TEMPLE

1 Corinthians 3:16
*Don't you realize that all of you together are the temple of
God and that the Spirit of God lives in you?*

In the Old Testament, the temple was the house of God. Believers went to the temple to meet with God and seek his favor and forgiveness through sacrifices. Many journeyed for several days over rough terrain to arrive at the place where God lived. Now all that has changed!

The sacrificial system of the Old Testament was completed for all time with the perfect sacrifice of the Lamb, Jesus Christ. Now there is favor and forgiveness for all who trust in Jesus as the One who died on their behalf and paid the penalty for their sins. Through Jesus we can have a personal relationship with the living God, a very personal relationship.

When people trust in Jesus as their Savior, the Holy Spirit takes up residence in their heart. The Spirit of God actually lives in us! We become the living, breathing houses of God. He will be in us and with us forever. The believer is significant because of the presence of God in him or her. Our identity is in Christ. We are secure. You are God's child forever!

*Father, thank you for the fact that your Holy Spirit lives in me.
Thank you for making me your temple, the place where you dwell.
Thank you for your promise that you will never move out of my
heart, your home. In Jesus' name. Amen.*

Personal Reflection:

_____

_____

_____

_____

_____

_____

_____

_____

_____

_____

_____

_____

_____

_____

_____

_____

_____

_____

_____

_____

_____

_____

VICTORY OVER SIN AND DEATH

1 Corinthians 15:54-57

Then, when our dying bodies have been transformed into bodies that will never die, this Scripture will be fulfilled: "Death is swallowed up in victory. O death, where is your victory? O death, where is your sting?" For sin is the sting that results in death, and the law gives sin its power. But thank God! He gives us victory over sin and death through our Lord Jesus Christ.

I watched my dad die. Cancer robbed him of energy and vigor, and left him lying in a bed, surrounded by his family watching him take his last breath. Death is not glorious. Paul describes it as the last enemy. However, it is a holy moment. I watched my dad pass from death to life.

I say that with confidence because of the truth in today's passage. My dad trusted in Jesus Christ alone as the only way to have a personal relationship with the living God. He did not trust in religious tradition or good deeds. He knew he was saved by grace through faith and not by works (Ephesians 2:8-9). My dad was not judged for his sins because Jesus had taken that judgment for him.

The Bible describes death as leaving one place and arriving in another. As one would cross over a bridge to get from one side of a river to the other, so the believer crosses over from this world to eternal life. This world is not our home. One day all of us will leave this earth. But with Jesus by our side, we will cross over and enter the place that has been prepared for us. Our peace comes from knowing that Jesus will be by our side all the way home.

Father, thank you for sending Jesus to build the great Cross Over.
Thank you for the peace that comes from knowing death is simply
a transition from this temporal life to life eternal.
In Jesus' name. Amen.

Personal Reflection:

_____

_____

_____

_____

_____

_____

_____

_____

_____

_____

_____

_____

_____

_____

_____

_____

_____

_____

COMPETENCE

2 Corinthians 3:4-5

We are confident of all this because of our great trust in God through Christ. It is not that we think we are qualified to do anything on our own. Our qualification comes from God.

The spiritual life is superhuman. The things God calls me to are beyond my capabilities. The tasks before me are outside my skill set. The spiritual journey outpaces my strength. Check out Paul's dose of reality in today's passage. We are not "competent in ourselves to claim anything for ourselves." Say it with me, "I am inadequate." When you admit that, things start getting good!

I will never be able to conjure up the confidence I need for the challenges ahead, but I don't have to. My confidence is not in myself; it is in Christ. In Christ I will have all I need to do all God is calling me to do. My competence comes from God.

The fear of inadequacy is the futile exercise of trusting in myself. If I stop there, I will always be stamped as insufficient. However, if I begin there and turn to Christ, he will give me the confidence and competence to climb my pole of fear to a new level on my spiritual journey. Say it with me, "My competence comes from God!"

Dear Father, thank you for addressing my inadequacy with your sufficiency, my fear with your confidence, and my deficiencies with your competence. In Jesus' name. Amen.

Personal Reflection:

_____

_____

_____

_____

_____

_____

_____

_____

_____

_____

_____

_____

_____

_____

_____

_____

_____

_____

_____

_____

_____

GOING HOME

2 Corinthians 5:6-8
So we are always confident, even though we know that as long as we live in these bodies we are not at home with the Lord. For we live by believing and not by seeing. Yes, we are fully confident, and would rather be away from these earthly bodies, for then we will be at home with the Lord.

What happens when you die? The soul sleeps? Time is spent in a holding place? Purgatory? Nothing? No, no, no, and absolutely no! The Bible is clear that when believers die, they pass from death to life in heaven. As Paul wrote in today's passage, when we are away from the body we are at home with the Lord.

This truth was proven right from the cross. As Jesus hung on the cross, two thieves were dying on either side of him. One remained defiant until death, but the other said, "Jesus, remember me when you come into your Kingdom." Jesus replied, "I assure you, today you will be with me in paradise" (Luke 23:42-43). Jesus had told his disciples that when he died he was going to the Father (John 16:10). Now Jesus told the repentant thief that he would go to the Father with him.

The soul is that part of us that makes us who we are. It's our character, passions, desires, commitments, values, will, and emotions. Our souls are housed, for the time being, in our bodies; but you know all about that sad story. Our bodies break, wear down, and eventually wear out, but not our souls! Our souls fly from our bodies to the arms of Jesus. He says, "Time to go home!" When we leave the body, we are at home with the Lord.

Father, thank you that death is the beginning not the end.
Thank you that our home is with you forever. Thank you for the gift
of grace through Jesus that provides the path for our journey home.
In his name we thank you. Amen.

Personal Reflection:

_____

_____

_____

_____

_____

_____

_____

_____

_____

_____

_____

_____

_____

_____

_____

_____

_____

ALL THAT WE NEED

2 Corinthians 9:8
And God will generously provide all you need. Then you will always have everything you need and plenty left over to share with others.

Many people live with a "scarcity" mind-set, a glass-half-empty philosophy that is always focused on the "What if this happens?" or "What if it doesn't happen?" The "scarcity" mind-set is not the needed process of risk management; it is the problem of being risk averse. "Scarcity" is always based in the fear of inadequacy. "We'll never have what we need." "We'll never measure up." "We'll never be able to satisfy."

Here is the truth of God's Word—He will always give you exactly what you need to do everything He calls you to do. If God is calling you to do something, the question you face is not about risk; it's about trust. Can you trust God to bless you abundantly? Can you trust God to give you all you need? Can God really be trusted to make sure you have "plenty left over to share with others."

The fear of inadequacy leaves God out of the picture. It is a self-focused fear that believes, "If it's to be, it's up to me." Let's face it, if it's up to me to make things happen, then nothing worthwhile is going to happen. The fear of inadequacy is real, but don't let it paralyze you. Let it be a reminder of how much you need God—the God who will in all things at all times, give you exactly what you need.

Father, help me face my fear of inadequacy. Remind me that you are able to bless abundantly. Please work in my life to turn fear into faith so that I can do all that you are calling me to do. In Jesus' name. Amen.

Personal Reflection:

_____

_____

_____

_____

_____

_____

_____

_____

_____

_____

_____

_____

_____

_____

_____

_____

_____

_____

_____

_____

_____

CHRIST'S POWER IN ME!

2 Corinthians 12:7-9

So to keep me from becoming proud, I was given a thorn in my flesh, a messenger from Satan to torment me and keep me from becoming proud. Three different times I begged the Lord to take it away. Each time he said, "My grace is all you need. My power works best in weakness." So now I am glad to boast about my weaknesses, so that the power of Christ can work through me.

Here is a powerful story from a friend of mine named Mike. It shows that God's grace is sufficient! His power is always made perfect in our weakness.

I often lean on 2 Corinthians 12:7-10. How Paul responds to his "thorn" taught me to deal with my thorn of cerebral palsy. Growing up, I had little experience with church, and what I did experience was bad. I was told my CP was a result of sin, demons, and a lack of faith. This made me feel rejected by God. For years, I prayed for healing and didn't understand why this thorn wouldn't go away. But despite bad doctrine being taught to me, Jesus saved me at 19; and in my study I came across these words: "My grace is sufficient for you, for my power is made perfect in weakness." Paul did not respond with a "woe is me" response when the Lord answered him this way. He rejoiced that Christ would get glory through his weakness. Jesus has taught me that human weakness is the perfect platform to display his glory. This is true with my cerebral palsy. The world and religion wrote me off. Doctors said that I would not do much with my life. Religion taught me that God rejected me. But Jesus taught me that he not only accepts me, but he was going to use my CP and my life to make much of him. I am a husband, father, minister, and former youth pastor. The doctors were right, I haven't done much with my life; Jesus has!

Father, thank you for Mike's story! Thank you for how you have used him and for teaching him that "human weakness is the perfect platform to display" your glory. Teach that lesson to us as well. In Jesus' name. Amen.

Personal Reflection:

UNDER CONSTRUCTION

Philippians 1:6
*And I am certain that God, who began the good work within
you, will continue his work until it is finally finished on
the day when Christ Jesus returns.*

All believers should wear a T-shirt that says UNDER
CONSTRUCTION. We are unfinished projects. God started a good
work in us, but he's not finished. He will "continue his work until it
is finished." It will be finished with our last breath.

The fear of insignificance settles in our hearts when we forget that
we are works in progress. During this life we'll have our share of
spiritual trips and falls. We'll take three spiritual steps forward, then
two back. We will disappoint others and ourselves.

Significance is nourished when I remember who I am and whose
I am. I am a child of God and will be forever! I know that God is
the One who started the spiritual work in my life. I know that he
will never leave any project unfinished. I am confident that God,
who began this work in my life, will deliver me completely because
of the finished work of Jesus. My significance is in Jesus. Any other
person will leave me incomplete.

*Lord Jesus, thank you for your finished work of salvation.
Thank you for starting that work in me, and thank you for
the certain promise that one day it will be completed
when I meet you face to face. Amen.*

Personal Reflection:

_____

_____

_____

_____

_____

_____

_____

_____

_____

_____

_____

_____

_____

_____

_____

_____

_____

_____

_____

_____

_____

PRESS ON!

Philippians 3:12

I don't mean to say that I have already achieved these things or that I have already reached perfection. But I press on to possess that perfection for which Christ Jesus first possessed me.

The great apostle Paul was a realist. He said, "I want to know Christ and experience the mighty power that raised him from the dead." Then he noted that he wasn't there yet; he had not "already achieved these things." Can you relate? You are not where you want to be in your spiritual journey.

What's holding you back? Could one thing be the fear of failing, or failing again? Maybe you've "gotten serious" about your walk with Christ before and made good progress—for a while—but then life got in the way and you fell back into the same old habits of disobedience. Now you're thinking, *What's the use? I don't want to fail again.*

Here's the newsbreak—you will fail again. Perfection will not occur in this life. Reread today's passage. Paul had not acquired what he wanted. He could not say, "Mission accomplished!" The Christian life is not the destination; it's the process. That's why we keep going. That's why we press on. One of these days we will arrive at our goal—heaven! Until then the dusty, winding, and challenging paths of life call us to press on.

Father, don't let us sit still, go back, or take a detour.
Help us press on. In Jesus' name. Amen.

Personal Reflection:

_____

_____

_____

_____

_____

_____

_____

_____

_____

_____

_____

_____

_____

_____

_____

_____

_____

_____

_____

_____

_____

_____

THE POWER OF PEACE

Philippians 4:6-7

Don't worry about anything; instead, pray about everything.
Tell God what you need, and thank him for all he has done.
Then you will experience God's peace, which exceeds anything
we can understand. His peace will guard your hearts
and minds as you live in Christ Jesus.

Don't worry. It's easier said than done, isn't it? Anxiety penetrates our hearts when we are ...

> ... waiting on the test results ...
> ... waiting on a teenager who is late coming home ...
> ... waiting to see if your job will be part of the downsizing ...
> ... trying to make ends meet ...
> ... wondering if he will stay with you or leave with her ...
> ... battling a barrage of "what ifs" ...

God's instruction on worry is not "Get ahold of yourself." Rather, God wants us to get ahold of him. Worry is the reminder to take our fears to God. Tell him that you're scared. Confess your doubts. Pour out your dread. Let him know your reservations. Thank God that he hears you and promises to meet you right where you are.

God promises that when we take our concerns to him, he will provide a stillness of the soul that surpasses all human understanding. This calmness will stand like armed guards around your heart and mind. Our anxious request is not a "one and done." It is a moment-by-moment, situation-by-situation, day-by-day continuance of presenting our needs to God; and he delivers with his power of peace.

Father, thank you for the promise of your peace. Help me use each anxious thought as a reminder to take my anxiety to you. Thank you for replacing the feeling of overwhelming anxiety with your calmness that goes beyond human understanding. In Jesus' name. Amen.

Personal Reflection:

_____

_____

_____

_____

_____

_____

_____

_____

_____

_____

_____

_____

_____

_____

_____

_____

_____

FOR THE JOURNEY

Philippians 4:12-13

I know how to live on almost nothing or with everything. I have learned the secret of living in every situation, whether it is with a full stomach or empty, with plenty or little. For I can do everything through Christ, who gives me strength.

The apostle Paul understood the range of life experiences. Check out his resume.

- Received 40 lashes—five times
- Beaten with rods—three times
- Shipwrecked—three times
- Stoned—one time
- Went without sleep
- Went without food
- Went without clothes in the cold

In summary, Paul said, "I have ... been put in prison ... been whipped ... and faced death again and again" (2 Corinthians 11:23). The great apostle understood what it was like to live in great need and to have plenty. Through it all he explained, "I can do everything through Christ, who gives me strength."

Whatever God calls us to do, he gives us the "can do." Whatever the situation, we can do what God wants us to do through his strength. Ability does not come from positive thinking. It comes from the power of the Spirit who lives in us. In every situation God provides his strength.

Father, thank you for providing strength for every assignment.
Thank you for the ability to do everything you call us to do.
In Jesus' name. Amen.

Personal Reflection:

_____

_____

_____

_____

_____

_____

_____

_____

_____

_____

_____

_____

_____

_____

_____

_____

_____

_____

_____

_____

_____

ALL MY NEEDS MET

Philippians 4:19
And this same God who takes care of me will supply all your needs from his glorious riches, which have been given to us in Christ Jesus.

What do you need to do the thing that God is calling you to do? What's holding you back? What's causing spiritual paralysis? What's causing you to run from God? What's the one thing you need to make you feel sufficient to follow hard after God?

Well, according to today's passage, the fear of inadequacy has a remedy. Seems to me this verse promises that God will meet all of your needs. He won't have to take out a loan. He will meet your needs according to his unlimited riches.

What's keeping you from asking God to meet all your needs so you can do what he's calling you to do? Could it be that you have become a bit too comfortable with your fear of inadequacy? Could it be that inadequacy has become your safe house? Could it be that your "Not me, Lord, I don't measure up" attitude has become your go-to excuse? A believer frozen by the fear of inadequacy is like a starving man sitting next to a pot of gold, content to starve with riches just a reach away.

Father, please give us a sample today of how your riches meet our needs. Then, with that taste of your promise, help us move forward with confidence and faith. In Jesus' name. Amen.

Personal Reflection:

_____

_____

_____

_____

_____

_____

_____

_____

_____

_____

_____

_____

_____

_____

_____

_____

_____

_____

_____

_____

_____

_____

I WILL RISE!

1 Thessalonians 4:14-16

For since we believe that Jesus died and was raised to life again, we also believe that when Jesus returns, God will bring back with him the believers who have died. We tell you this directly from the Lord: We who are still living when the Lord returns will not meet him ahead of those who have died. For the Lord himself will come down from heaven with a commanding shout, with the voice of the archangel, and with the trumpet call of God. First, the Christians who have died will rise from their graves.

What happens when we die? Do we enter the grave in a sort of soul sleep until Jesus returns? Do we live as spirits forever? Will we be able to recognize each other? Let's consider these questions.

- Our souls—man's spirit that lives inside the body—will cross over from death to life (John 5:24). When we (our souls) are absent from the body, we will be present with the Lord (2 Corinthians 5:6-8).

- At death our bodies will be interred, awaiting the resurrection of the dead.

- When Jesus comes again, God will send believers who have died ("fallen asleep") with him (1 Thessalonians 4:14).

- Then the "believer who have died will rise from their graves." Our bodies will rise from the grave and meet the Lord in the air to join with our spirits, and we will be with the Lord forever (1 Thessalonians 4:16b).

Forever in heaven we will live in our recognizable, resurrected bodies, just like Jesus. We will delight in indescribable joy as we live life eternal, praising God, enjoying each other, and doing the eternal work that God prepared for us to do. Nothing can defeat the believer. Nothing can hold us down. Not even the grave! We will rise!

Heavenly Father, thank you for this promise of resurrection. Thank you that when we know Jesus as our Savior, absolutely nothing can hold us back or hold us down. May we live today with the peace, confidence, and joy of those who will live forever. In Jesus' name. Amen.

Personal Reflection:

THE LORD IS MY HELPER

Hebrews 13:5-6

Don't love money; be satisfied with what you have. For God has said, "I will never fail you. I will never abandon you." So we can say with confidence, "The LORD is my helper, so I will have no fear. What can mere people do to me?"

The search for a life of confidence is on. Some move from relationship to relationship looking for a sense of peace in a person. Some try to find something to soothe their soul in a bottle, needle, or pill. The recipients of today's passage must have been putting their trust in the "Almighty Dollar"—the other god. The writer tells them to steer clear of money worship and learn contentment.

The writer to the Hebrews gives us this foundational truth: Confidence comes from one source—the person of Jesus. He is always with us. He will never leave us and never leaves us alone. He is the One who comes to our aid and stands by our side. He is our protection from the people and things that attack us.

Fear comes from being alone and vulnerable. Fear wells up within us when we feel we are helpless and life is out of control. However, when we understand who God is and believe his promises, we can say with confidence, "The LORD is my helper, so I will have no fear."

Lord Jesus, this is my profession: You are my helper; I will have no fear! Thank you for never leaving me alone. Amen.

Personal Reflection:

LIFE SURRENDER:
SPIRITUAL HEALING

1 Peter 2:24
"He personally carried our sins in his body on the cross so that we can be dead to sin and live for what is right. By his wounds you are healed."

The human heart is caught in a contradiction. On one hand, God has placed eternity in our hearts, leaving us with a God-shaped hole. We suffer from an inward famine. We are starving for God. On the other hand, we want to be our own god, call our own shots, be in control of our lives. We are afraid to surrender.

Our fear takes us on a quest to find fulfillment and satisfaction. Like the old song says, we are looking for love in all the wrong places. Everything we do to try to reach our destination leaves our hearts just as empty and hungry as when we began. We need God, but we want to be our own god. We are afraid to surrender.

Is your fear of surrender keeping you from God? Look at today's passage. Jesus carrier your sins in his body on the cross so that we could die to sin—surrender—and live for righteousness. It's time to stop running. Healing comes by the wounds and the work of Jesus on the cross. I invite you to pray the following prayer.

Father, I am tired of running. I am tired of being afraid. I am tired of trying to fill the hole in my heart with the stuff of this world. Right now I surrender. I trust in Jesus who carried my sins in his body on the cross. I want to die to my sin and live for you. I want to be healed by the work of Jesus. Please take away my fear and help me to surrender. In Jesus' name. Amen.

Personal Reflection:

_____

_____

_____

_____

_____

_____

_____

_____

_____

_____

_____

_____

_____

_____

_____

_____

_____

_____

_____

_____

_____

_____

_____

_____

ALL YOUR ANXIETY ON HIM

1 Peter 5:6-7

So humble yourselves under the mighty power of God, and at the right time he will lift you up in honor. Give all your worries and cares to God, for he cares about you.

It was a particularly hot day in Dallas, and I was driving around the city looking for an apartment. Having just graduated from seminary, Lori and I needed to move from the condo we had rented for four years. I had resumes scattered throughout the country but was getting no response, or rather I was getting a response —"No." We thought we would be looking for a place to live and minister in another part of the country; but, for the time being, we were staying in Dallas. It was a discouraging stretch of my journey.

These were the days before God blessed us with children, but for some reason there was a Psalty, the songbook cassette, left in our car left after a visit from Lori's sisters or my nieces. The Psalty series was a children's Christian "musical." I inserted the tape and heard Psalty sing, "I cast all my cares upon you. I lay all of my burdens down at your feet. And any time I don't know what to do, I will cast all my cares upon you." With tears in my eyes, I played that song, based on today's passage, over and over again. I had just finished four years of Greek, Hebrew, Bible, and Theology courses, but it was a children's song that delivered a needed promise of Scripture right to my heart.

I will never forget that day. God cared enough for me that he orchestrated someone leaving a tape behind in order to tenderly teach me that I could throw all my frustration, fear, and anxiety on him. If you are on a discouraging stretch of the journey, you have to know what I was reminded of that day—God really does care for you … he really does.

Father, thank you for reminding me of your care on that hot day in Dallas. Remind those reading this devotional of your care as well. In Jesus' name. Amen.

Personal Reflection:

_____

_____

_____

_____

_____

_____

_____

_____

_____

_____

_____

_____

_____

_____

_____

_____

_____

_____